The complete guide to

INTERNATIONAL FINANCIAL REPORTING STANDARDS

Including IAS and Interpretation

Second Edition

Ralph Tiffin

THOROGOOD

Published by Thorogood
10-12 Rivington Street
London EC2A 3DU

Telephone: 020 7749 4748
Fax: 020 7729 6110
Email: info@thorogood.ws
Web: www.thorogood.ws

Books Network International Inc
3 Front Street, Suite 331
Rollinsford, NH 30869, USA

Telephone: +603 749 9171
Fax: +603 749 6155
Email: bizbks@aol.com

© Ralph Tiffin 2005

A CIP catalogue record for this book is available
from the British Library.

ISBN 1 85418 337 0

Cover and book designed in the UK
by Driftdesign

Printed in India by Replika Press

Special discounts for bulk
quantities of Thorogood
books are available to
corporations, institutions,
associations and other
organisations. For more
information contact
Thorogood by telephone
on 020 7749 4748, by fax on
020 7729 6110, or e-mail us:
info@thorogood.ws

Dedication

To my friend A

Acknowledgement

I would like to thank David Young for his support and valued contribution in preparing this text.

This book is an aid to understanding the purpose of IFRS's, the principal accounting and disclosure issues and problem areas. To ensure proper and detailed application of the Standards it will be necessary to refer to the Standards, authoritative supporting pronouncements and possibly seek appropriate expert opinion.

Contents

Introduction

Accounting, used in this context to mean the recording and presentation of business events in traditional financial statements (the balance sheet and profit & loss account), is believed by many to be an exact science.

For many accountants, rules (though not all written down), convention and practice mean that events will always be recorded correctly and presented fairly. However, there are genuine differences in opinion as to both how events may be recorded and presented. There is also the possibility of distorting both the recording and the presentation. Finally, there is the question of what transactions and events should be included in each set of financial statements.

Thus there are fundamental reasons for the existence and application of Accounting Standards. There is the need for consistency throughout the business world, the prevention of misleading presentation and disclosure of events.

The purpose of this text

The purpose of this text is to explain in as clear and simple terms as possible the principles of extant International Accounting Standards (IAS). These are being re-titled International Financial Reporting Standards (IFRS) as new Standards are introduced. The reasons for Accounting Standards are explained under the background to the Standards.

The text is aimed at: anyone in business who has to interface with published accounts and internal reports; anyone who is responsible for reports that are affected by or lead to published accounts. As never before, professional advisers, directors and executive officers from functions other than finance are affected by the requirements of Accounting Standards. Accountants and students of accountancy will also find this text useful as a summary of Accounting Standards, as it cuts through to exactly what the Standards aim to achieve and thus what has to be accounted for and disclosed.

Method of study and order of the sections

This text is not a re-write of the Standards but rather summarizes the issues which give rise to the Standard practice, explaining the accounting and disclosure requirements and practical problems of compliance. For those who wish to review financial statements, terminology and measures there is a chapter covering; the format and content of principal financial statements, commonly used performance measures and how these can be distorted by improper accounting practice. Even accountants who are used to such matters may find these chapters a good reminder of some of the essentially simple issues with which Accounting Standards aim to deal.

Why do we need Accounting Standards?

There are different views on how to account for and report business transactions. These may be due to cultural or commercial reasons or because of legislative or taxation laws.

A prime aim of Standards is to bring consistency of reporting within and between countries. Investors and others using financial statements (e.g. for investing or benchmarking purposes) can then make decisions based on consistently prepared data.

However, consistency is not the only reason that Standards are needed. There can be poor or down right bad accounting. Poor accounting may mean lack of exactness giving a wide range of values or inadequate disclosure. Bad accounting could mean fraud.

Why do YOU need to understand Accounting Standards?

Owners, directors, managers and professional advisers, such as lawyers, have a responsibility to understand how business activities are presented in the financial statements – what is going on in the business.

The accounting ideas behind them and the effect on financial statements of each of the Standards are explained.

Format of the section covering each Standard

Why needed

What the accounting/reporting issues are and the aims of the Standard.

Ideas – concepts

An explanation, in simple terms of what the accounting and or presentation issues are.

Key terms

Key definitions: they come from either the International Standard or, where helpful in explaining ideas and concepts, from the UK Standards. Note that the issue of standardising definitions is one that has to be addressed during the harmonisation of world Standards.

Required accounting/disclosure

Where appropriate the method of accounting for an item is explained in clear terms.

What has to be disclosed?

Problem areas and questions to ask about the accounts

The acknowledged or latent problems that may be encountered when applying the Standards. Matters that should be discussed before approving financial statements that will comply with the Standards.

A note of really significant differences in UK GAAP (Generally Accepted Accounting Practices).

Objectives and further definitions from the Standard

THE OBJECTIVE OF THE STANDARD AS SET OUT IN THE STANDARD.

The commentary on each Standard includes the objective written for each Standard by the Standard setters. It is obvious with both the International and UK Standards that there were different authors. The style varies considerably. Some are clear and to the point, others ramble on, and for some Standards no objective exists. They are included because they can help to explain what the issues are and why the Standard is needed. The 'Why needed' introduction aims to succinctly set out the objectives.

Barriers to understanding

Terminology

A barrier to understanding accounting is the differing terminology and statement layouts commonly used. Whilst there has been some success in, for example, Standardising EU financial statement terminology and layouts (appropriately translated), there remains much diversity. Accounting Standards should drive further Standardisation in the use of words and statement layout but different practices will remain. This is due to differences in custom, cultural differences or the sloppy use of English. An example is:

- In the UK we say stock, in the US and under IAS it would be inventory.

In this text the words from the Standards are used as far as possible, but common UK terminology is also frequently used. Thus profit & loss account is used as well as income statement; business or company, as well as entity. Thought was given to using only the IAS 'word' but in practice readers will need to contend with different terminology. The everyday words are often synonymous but there may be subtleties in different word usage.

Lesson: If in doubt check exactly how a word is being used.

Understanding financial statement and accounting practices

Further support to your understanding the Standards can be found at the end of the book where there are review chapters. What balance sheets, profit and loss accounts (income or earnings statements) and cash flow statements aim to convey. The effect of the principal different national differences in components and layouts is explained. The use of financial statements as a basis or interpreting a business by carrying out ratio analysis is also outlined. Finally, the effect on analysis through distortions in accounting method and layout is demonstrated by examples of 'creative accounting'.

Order of chapters

The majority of Accounting Standards were issued in response to an event – a significant lapse in proper accounting and disclosure. Thus the chronological or numerical order of the Standards is illogical (in any event it is questionable as to whether academics or practitioners could agree to a logical order). The history of the development of individual Accounting Standards often illustrates why Standards are needed.

The Standards are dealt with in the following groupings, the aim being to make the study of the Accounting Standards more coherent. If a particular Standard or issue has to be understood then the table below or the numerical index should lead the reader to the topic.

- Financial statement formats and contents
- Accounting methods and conventions
- Creative accounting*
- Disclosure (of significant information)
- Accounting for groups and investments
- Specialized industries
- Other

* The section Creative Accounting may imply that this is allowed – it is NOT. A principal reason for Standards is to prevent such practices. Without Standards these aspects of accounting may be particularly susceptible to abuse.

ONE

Summary objectives and requirements of the Standards

1.1

Accounting policies, financial statement formats and content

IAS 1 – Presentation of financial statements

Financial statements should have standard minimum content and the bases on which the figures are prepared should be explained.

The Standard sets out the minimum contents of financial statements: balance sheet, income statement, cash flow statement, significant accounting policies, statement of changes in equity and supporting notes where appropriate.

The Standard reiterates the fundamental accounting concepts of going concern and accruals and their place in the accounting framework.

IAS 8 – Accounting policies, changes in accounting estimates and errors
IFRS 5 – Non-current assets held for sale and discontinued operations

Profits and losses should generally be taken to the income statement with any large one-off items disclosed separately, particularly the effects of discontinuing operations.

The Standards require the disclosure of material one-off items, including the costs of discontinuing operations. Non-current (fixed) assets that are to be sold should be disclosed separately.

Also the reporting of errors or alterations to the figures due to changes in accounting policies should be disclosed.

IAS 7- Cash flow statements

Cash flow statements should present the business from the perspective of how it generates and consumes cash and how it is funded.

The Standard requires details of historical changes in cash and cash equivalents of an enterprise by means of a statement which classifies cash flows during the period from operating, investing and financing activities.

IAS 34 – Interim financial reporting

Interim financial reports must contain a minimum amount of reliable information.

The Standard requires that interim financial statements should contain the same individual reports and use the same accounting policies as the annual statutory accounts. It may be practical and acceptable to demand less detail in some of the disclosures and notes.

IFRS 1 – First time application of IAS's

Businesses adopting IFRS's should comply with them.

The Standard requires an entity to use the same (IFRS compliant) accounting policies in its opening IFRS balance sheet and throughout all periods presented in its first IFRS financial statements.

Accounting methods and conventions

IAS 16 – Property plant and equipment

Tangible fixed assets are a major part of capital employed for the many businesses. They should be carried at cost, or if revalued then this should be done so on a consistent basis.

The Standard codifies much of existing accounting practice. Assets may be carried at cost or revalued. Fixed assets (except land) should be depreciated over reasonable periods.

IAS 40 – Investment property

Investment properties are held for gain, not consumption. It is inappropriate to depreciated them, but they should be revalued to up to date fair value.

The Standard requires that investment properties should not be depreciated but shown at fair value.

IAS 38 – Intangible assets

Intangible assets are important for many businesses and in spite of difficulties in valuing them they should be recognized in the balance sheet as assets at cost. The cost should be amortized over reasonable periods or checked annually for impairment in value.

The Standard requires that purchased goodwill and intangible assets are capitalized at cost but reviewed annually for impairment. Own generated intangibles such as brands, patents etc. must not be capitalized in the balance sheet.

IAS 36 – Impairment of assets

There is a need to have some 'science' to ensure assets carried in the balance sheet at fair value have not lost value due to changes in economic circumstances. This Standard aims to provide the framework for prudently valuing goodwill, intangibles and also tangible fixed assets.

The Standard requires a review for impairment of a fixed asset or goodwill to be carried out if events, or changes in circumstances, indicate that the carrying amount of the fixed asset or goodwill may not be recoverable.

Then if, and only if, the recoverable amount of an asset is less than its carrying amount, its carrying amount should be reduced to its recoverable amount. The resultant impairment loss which should be recognized in the income statement or against any previous revaluation of the same asset.

IAS 2 – Inventories/stock

Stock and short-term work in progress values are critical to the reporting of profits or losses at the correct amount and in the correct period. Clear definition of terms and defined accounting is required.

The Standard requires that inventories/stock be valued at cost or net realizable value. The method of measuring stock should be to value each item at historical cost, or as close an approximation as is possible.

IAS 11 – Construction contracts/Long-term WIP

The valuation of construction contracts or long-term work in progress is critical to the reporting of balance sheet values and profits or losses – definition of terms and defined accounting is required.

The Standard requires that when the outcome of a construction contract can be estimated with reasonable reliability, revenue and costs should be recognized by reference to the stage of construction. If it is probable that total costs will exceed total revenue the expected contract loss should be recognized as an expense immediately. The amounts of revenue from contracts and the method of recognising this revenue should be disclosed.

IAS 37 – Provisions, contingent liabilities and contingent assets

Provisions should be made only when there is certainty of a future liability. Other potential but nebulous liabilities (or assets) should be quantified and disclosed as contingent liabilities.

The Standard accepts the business and commercial need for provisions but brings definition as to when and how provisions should be sanctioned. The

Standard demands a high degree of certainty as to cause and amount before provisions can be made.

IAS 21 – The effects of changes in foreign exchange rates

Currency gains and losses can be realized or unrealized, many different rates could be used for translation purposes, and gains or losses could be shown in different places in the accounts.

The Standard requires that transactions should be translated at the rate ruling at the date of the transaction. Balance sheet figures should be translated at the rate ruling at the balance sheet date. For non-monetary assets and liabilities the historical rate should be used.

IAS 12 – Income taxes/current tax/deferred tax

An explanation of the bases for tax charges or credits and where they are recognized in the financial statements is needed. Provision should be made for future tax liabilities that will arise on the reversal of timing differences between accounts and tax charges.

The Standard requires an explanation of the relationship between tax expense or income and accounting profit. It also requires an explanation of changes in the applicable tax rate(s) compared with the previous accounting period.

The Standard requires that a deferred tax liability should be recognized for all taxable temporary differences and charged to the income statement. A deferred tax asset should be recognized to the extent that it is probable that taxable profit will be available in the future against which to recover tax or reduce liability.

IAS 19 – Employee benefits

The cost of employee benefits to a business should be disclosed, particularly the cost of pension liabilities.

The Standard requires disclosure of all significant classes of employee benefits, but particularly pension contributions.

The Standard requires disclosure of contributions to both defined contribution and defined benefit schemes. For defined benefit schemes the adequacy of funding has to be calculated and any liability due to under-funding disclosed.

1.3
Creative accounting

IAS 18 – Revenue

The primary issue in accounting for revenue is determining when to recognize revenue – when sales have been irrevocably earned.

The Standard requires that revenue only be recognized when quantifiable inflows (of cash) will definitely occur. The Standard identifies the circumstances by which these criteria will be met and, therefore, revenue can be recognized. It also provides practical guidance on the application of the criteria.

IAS 17 – Leases

The substance of what is going on in business is more important than simply reporting the legal form of transactions. A commitment to make payments for a number of years for the use of an asset means you effectively own the asset BUT also have the contra liability.

The Standard requires that leased, hired or rented assets should be shown as assets of the lessee along with the related liability – the obligation to make lease payments.

IAS 23 – Borrowing costs

Borrowing costs relate to funding businesses and should be charged against income as incurred. However, fixed assets often require considerable funds to finance their construction. Borrowing or interest costs may be considered a cost specifically incurred to bring the asset into revenue earning condition – under strict conditions the costs may be capitalized.

The Standard requires that borrowing costs should be recognized as an expense as they are incurred except to the extent that they are directly attributable to acquisition, construction or production of a fixed asset.

IAS 20 – Accounting for government grants

Grants may be given to support day to day operations – revenue, or to encourage investment in fixed assets – capital. The correct classification is important.

The Standard requires the correct matching of grant credits either as revenue items or capital items. Specifically, capital grants (for equipment etc.) should be spread over the life of the asset and not taken as income.

IFRS 2 – Shared Based Payment

Entities often grant shares or share options to employees or other parties. With out calculation of the cost of the payment and full disclosure of long term effects such payments may appear 'free'. Awarding shares or share options means that a portion of the value of the company is being given away.

The standard requires that a value is put on the cost of awarding share based payments and that the cost is recognised immediately in profit and loss.

1.4
Disclosure

IAS 10 – Events occurring after the balance sheet date

Events may affect a company after the year end but before accounts are 'signed off'. Events may not cause change to figures in the financial statements, however, to ignore them may be misleading to users of the financial statements.

The Standard requires that significant events after the balance sheet date should be reported by way of note(s) to the accounts.

IAS 24 – Related party disclosures

Who really owns and controls the business? This is vital information if all those involved with the business are to be treated fairly.

The Standard requires disclosure of who really owns and controls the business (related parties) along with details of transactions and balances between the business and these related parties.

IAS 33 – Earnings per share

An earnings per share ratio is considered an important ratio. If there was no clear definition then this ratio could be miss-presented.

This Standard prescribes the basis for calculating and presenting earnings and other amounts per share in the financial statements of publicly quoted entities.

IAS 32 – Financial instruments: Disclosure and presentation

IAS 39 – Financial Instruments: Recognition and measurement

What is debt (loans) and what is equity (risk capital)? What financial risks has a business entered into by dealing in derivatives – hedges, futures etc?

The Standards aim to define what is not equity.

The Standards require disclosure of information that can help identify the risks a business has in respect of financial instruments.

Where possible financial assets should be revalued to fair value at the balance sheet date.

Hedging (netting of gains and losses) is allowed under strict conditions.

1.5

Accounting for groups and investments

IFRS 3 – Business combinations

IAS 27 – Consolidated and separate financial statements

Businesses acquire other businesses – acquisitions. The difference between purchase price and fair value of assets acquired is goodwill which should be disclosed in the balance sheet of the group, carried at cost, but tested each year for any impairment.

The Standards imply that acquisition accounting with the calculation and disclosure of goodwill should be the norm. Consolidated group accounts should be produced. Merger accounting is prohibited.

The Standards aim to define at what date an acquisition should be accounted for. Values used should be fair values and any resulting goodwill should be carried at cost, tested for impairment but NOT written off over a number of years.

IAS 28 – Accounting for investments in associates

IAS 31 – Financial reporting of interests in joint ventures

A company could own 1%, 14%, 38% etc. of another company. The issue is how should the net assets and results of these different levels of ownership be accounted for? Definition is needed for the varying levels of investment and control.

The Standards define the treatment of a business's investments in other companies. There needs to be a clear and consistently applied distinction between control (a subsidiary) and other levels of investment and influence on the owned entity.

IAS 14 – Segment reporting

An important use of financial statements is to identify performance and the amount of, and existence of, assets and liabilities. Some analysis of the overall picture is required.

The Standard aims to assist analysis of a diverse group's business activities by requiring a breakdown of key figures in the balance sheet and income statement on geographical and business classification bases.

1.6
Specialized industries

IAS 26 – Accounting and reporting by retirement benefit plans

Employees (prospective pensioners) and existing pensioners need to know whether a business's pension scheme is adequately funded. The accounts of such funds should clearly and fairly state the basis on which assets and liabilities are recognized and valued in the scheme's balance sheet.

The Standard requires the following disclosures:

- For a defined contributions scheme a statement of the funding policy, a summary of significant accounting policies and net assets available for benefits.

- For defined benefit plans a statement of net assets available for benefits and the actuarial present value of promised retirement benefits and thus the resulting surplus or deficit of the plan's fund.

IAS 30 – Disclosure in financial statements of banks and similar financial institutions

For banks there are internationally agreed minimum levels of shareholders' equity, and profiles of loans – the Basle Convention rules. To enable regulators, investors and customers to confirm that banks are sound financially requires proper disclosure in amount and particularly, classification of liabilities and assets.

The Standard aims to ensure proper disclosure of the necessary information – specific accounting policies and the principal amounts of income and expenses under appropriate headings should be disclosed.

IAS 41 – Agriculture

Agriculture is a specialized area of business and thus accounting is specialized. An issue is the valuation of livestock and crops.

The Standard requires that a biological asset should be measured on initial recognition and thereafter at its fair value, and appropriate accounting policies should be disclosed.

IFRS 4 – Insurance Contracts

Accounting practices for insurance contracts have been diverse, and have often differed from practices in other sectors. This standard is a first phase aimed at improving accounting for insurance and requiring disclosure of information about such contracts.

The approach of this initial standard covering the insurance contracts is to align accounting with that set out in the IFRS framework, prohibit what is unacceptable practice and move accounting policies and disclosure towards what is considered best practice.

The three principal aims of the standards are to:

- Improve accounting policies and ensure they align with the Framework
- Carry out liability adequacy tests and if there is a shortfall the entire amount should be recognized as a charge in profit and loss.
- Require disclosure about the amount, timing and uncertainty of future cash flows.

IFRS 6 – Exploration for and evaluation of mineral resources

There are differing views as to how exploration and evaluation expenditures should be accounted for. Thus there is need for a single acceptable approach, consistent with the IFRS framework and other existing IFRS's.

The standard gives general guidance, permitting capitalisation of expenses associated with exploring and evaluating mineral resources. It permits existing accounting policies to be continued but does point to possibly improved disclosure. It specifically requires that any expenses capitalised as assets should be subject to impairment reviews and gives outline example of signs of impairment.

1.7
Other

IAS 29 – Financial reporting in hyper inflationary economies

Economies can be subject to periods of hyper inflation. The problem is how to meaningfully report business results.

The Standard requires that figures for the period in question should be adjusted as at the year end balance sheet date, either by adjusting the historic cost figures with indices that adjust to the measuring unit (or currency), or by adjusting relevant balance sheet and earnings statement figures to current cost.

TWO
Statement formats and content

Presentation of financial statements – IAS 1

Why needed

What should a set of Financial Statements contain? There will be differing views as to what are essential to statements and their layout. This Standard lists the essential elements of a set of financial statements.

Also businesses must have clearly stated accounting policies (rules) if financial statements are to be read or interpreted clearly. Figures are meaningless if not prepared on a defined base. Accounting concepts such as 'going concern' and 'accruals' are considered fundamental or 'bedrock'. These and other concepts are defined and explained. If there were no rules then creative accounting might follow!

Ideas – concepts

Financial statements could contain endless statements, data and explanations. What is required is a practical minimum number of statements and narrative that permit a fair understanding of the financial results, cash flows and state of a business for a defined period.

A complete set of financial statements is considered to comprise:

- **a balance sheet**
- **an income statement** (P&L account)
- **a cash flow statement**

- **accounting policies** and explanatory notes
- **a statement of changes in equity** – all changes in equity or at least the changes that arise from capital transactions other than those with owners, e.g. revaluation gains.

Examples of balance sheets and income statements (and their differing national layouts) can be found in chapter 9. Cash flow statements, their content and layout can be found in IAS 7 and in chapter 2.5.

A statement of changes in equity should show all items that affect total shareholders' equity. That is profit or loss for the period, other gains or losses, adjustments due to changes in accounting policies, capital transactions with the owners, e.g. dividend payments or capital introduced. For many companies this is a very straightforward statement – opening amount, add profit for year less dividends gives closing amount.

Accounting policies define the process whereby transactions and other events are reflected in financial statements. Figures are meaningless if not prepared on a defined base. Accounting concepts such as 'going concern' and 'accruals' are considered fundamental or 'bedrock' and other concepts and desirable qualities and their application, are considered in this Standard or the IASB Framework. Policies are the particular ways in which concepts are applied to separate items in the financial statements.

For example, an accounting policy for a particular type of expenditure may specify whether an asset or an expense is to be recognized; the basis on which it is to be measured; and where in the balance sheet or income statement it is to be presented.

Key terms – The two fundamental or 'bedrock' concepts

GOING CONCERN

The preparer (and auditor) of the accounts should consider and check whether or not the enterprise is likely to continue in operational existence for the foreseeable future. This means, in particular, that there is no intention or necessity to liquidate or curtail significantly the scale of operations, and thus the balance sheet and income statement will not be materially affected.

The concept also requires the preparer (and auditor) to consider and check that the business is likely to have cash/bank resources sufficient to remain in business for the foreseeable future – 'foreseeable future' is considered by auditing Standards to be a period of at least twelve months beyond the date of signing the financial statements. When financial statements cannot or are not prepared on a going concern basis, then that fact should be disclosed.

ACCRUALS OR MATCHING CONCEPT

Revenue and costs should be accrued (that is, recognized as they are earned or incurred, not as money is received or paid), matched with one another so far as their relationship can be established or justifiably assumed, and dealt with in the income statement of the period to which they relate.

Other concepts and desirable qualities

CONSISTENCY

Presentation and classification of items in the financial statements should be retained from one period to the next, unless a more appropriate presentation evolves, e.g. due to business changes or because of an IFRS. Any change or inconsistency should be disclosed and quantified.

PRUDENCE

Prudence means being cautious. Prudence is the inclusion of a degree of caution in the exercise of judgment needed in making the estimates required under conditions of uncertainty, such that assets or expenses are not overstated and liabilities or expenses are not understated. However, the exercise of prudence does not allow the creation of hidden reserves.

SUBSTANCE OVER FORM

If financial statements are to represent events fairly then it is necessary that the substance or commercial reality of events is disclosed and not merely the legal form. A good example of abuse of this concept was Enron. Owning directly only a small percentage of 'subsidiaries' might keep assets and, more importantly, liabilities off Enron's balance sheet, but commercial reality was that these assets and liabilities were owned and controlled by Enron.

MATERIALITY AND AGGREGATION

Every material item should be presented separately and conversely imma-terial amounts should be aggregated with similar items.

OFF-SETTING OR NETTING OFF

Asset/liabilities and income/expenditure should not be off-set or netted off unless amounts are immaterial or an IFRS permits this action.

FAIR PRESENTATION

Financial statements should present fairly the financial position, performance and cash flows of a business. A specific example of the application of the 'fairness' principal is the concept of 'substance over form' as defined in the IASB Frame-work. If information is to represent faithfully the transactions and other events that it purports to represent, it is necessary that they are accounted for and presented in accordance with their substance and economic reality, and not merely their legal form. It may be reasonably assumed that complying with all IFRS's will result in fair presentation.

Accounting

The figures reported in financial statements should be compiled and presented as required by the appropriate Accounting Standard (if one exists). In any event figures should be compiled and presented based on the bedrock concepts of going concern and accruals, also taking into account the further issues and concepts set out in the IASB framework.

Disclosure

CONTENT OF FINANCIAL STATEMENTS

A balance sheet, income statement (P&L account)*, cash flow statement, state-ment of change in equity and accounting policies must be produced. The format of the statements will follow the IFRS recommendations of the layouts or as amended by local legislation, e.g. the EU has standardized layout and termi-nology for balance sheets and P&L accounts. See chapter 9.1 for examples.)

* **NOTE**: there is a firm proposal to combine the income statement/P&L account with a Statement of Total Recognized Gains and Losses to form a Statement of Financial Performance.

This statement will be divided into three sections:

1 Operating

2 Finance and treasury

3 Other gains and losses

Recycling of gains and losses between different sections of the performance statement is not permitted. Dividends for the period are excluded from the performance statement as they represent transactions with owners as owners rather than expenses. A reconciliation of ownership interests – a statement of changes in equity would still be required to be presented as a primary statement.

ACCOUNTING POLICIES

All significant accounting policies should be disclosed. **Also the judgements made by management in applying the accounting policies that have a (the most) significant effect on the amounts of items recognized in the financial statements.**

Key measurement assumptions

An entity shall disclose in the notes information regarding key assumptions about the future, and other sources of measurement uncertainty that have a significant risk of causing a material adjustment to the carrying amounts of assets and liabilities within the next financial year.

RESPONSIBILITY FOR FINANCIAL STATEMENTS

Acknowledgment of responsibility for Financial Statements is required – they are the responsibility of the board of directors or other governing body.

Problem areas and questions to ask about the accounts

STATEMENT LAYOUTS

Dealing with different layouts of statements – the ordering of lists of assets, liabilities etc., means that some homework often has to be done. Within a multinational business there should be a standard layout for internal and external reporting.

NON-COMPLIANCE WITH STANDARDS

In the extremely rare situation when compliance with an IAS is considered to be misleading then the departure from the Standard necessary to achieve a fair (in the UK true and fair) presentation is permitted. Disclosures should include:

- that management concluded that the financial statements (with the non-compliance) do fairly present position, cash flows and performance;

- that all other relevant Standards have been complied with;

- the nature of and rationale for departure from a Standard; and

- the financial impact of non-compliance on the profit and net assets of the enterprise.

SIGNIFICANT DIFFERENCES IN GAAP

The only significant key differences are in the layouts and terminology of financial statements in different countries.

Objective and definitions from the Standard

Objective

The objective of this Standard is to prescribe the basis for presentation of general purpose financial statements, in order to ensure comparability both with the enterprise's own financial statements of previous periods, and with the financial statements of other enterprises. To achieve this objective, this Standard sets out overall considerations for the presentation of financial statements, guidelines for their structure and minimum requirements for the content. The recognition, measurement and disclosure of specific transactions and events are dealt with in other Standards.

Definitions

Impracticable Applying a requirement is impracticable when the entity cannot apply it after making every reasonable effort to do so.

International Financial Reporting Standards (IFRSs) are Standards and Interpretations adopted by the International Accounting Standards Board (IASB).

They comprise:

a) International Financial Reporting Standards;

b) International Accounting Standards; and

c) Interpretations originated by the International Financial Reporting Interpretations Committee (IFRIC) or the former Standing Interpretations Committee (SIC).

Material Omissions or misstatements of items are material if they could, individually or collectively, influence the economic decisions of users taken on the basis of the financial statements. Materiality depends on the size and nature of the omission or misstatement judged in the surrounding circumstances. The size or nature of the item, or a combination of both, could be the determining factor.

Notes contain information in addition to that presented in the balance sheet, income statement, statement of changes in equity and cash flow statement. Notes provide narrative descriptions or disaggregations of items disclosed in those statements and information about items that do not qualify for recognition in those statements.

GOING CONCERN

When preparing financial statements, management shall make an assessment of the enterprise's ability to continue as a going concern. Financial statements shall be prepared on a going concern basis unless management either intends to liquidate the entity or to cease trading, or has no realistic alternative but to do so. When management is aware, in making its assessment, of material uncertainties related to events or conditions which may cast significant doubt upon the enterprise's ability to continue as a going concern, those uncertainties should be disclosed. When the financial statements are not prepared on a going concern basis, that fact should be disclosed, together with the basis on which the financial statements are prepared and the reason why the entity is not considered to be a going concern.

ACCRUAL BASIS OF ACCOUNTING

Under the accrual basis of accounting, transactions and events are recognized when they occur (and not as cash or its equivalent is received or paid), and they are recorded in the accounting records and reported in the financial statements of the periods to which they relate. Expenses are recognized in the income statement on the basis of a direct association between the costs incurred and the earning of specific items of income (matching). However, the application of the matching concept does not allow the recognition of items in the balance sheet which do not meet the definition of assets or liabilities.

2.2

Accounting policies, changes in accounting estimates and errors – IAS 8

Why needed

What is the bottom line? Good question! Are one off profits to be included? If a business acquires and disposes of activities how is the underlying core business doing? Results need to be disclosed in their constituent parts.

What is the bottom line? Should all income/expense be included in the calculation of profit? What is **net** profit?

Are income/expenses exceptional or extraordinary?

How should changes in profit due to changes in accounting methods/policies be reported?

This revised Standard now focuses on the last issue – accounting policies and changes in estimates and dealing with errors – and aims to answer these questions.

It should be noted that this Standard along with IAS's 1 – Presentation of Financial Statements may be supplanted with a new Standard that embraces many of the issues that arise in reporting the components of profit or loss.

Ideas – concepts

Businesses make profits or losses from their core, continuing businesses, but also will have profits or losses from exceptional, unusual or extraordinary sources. These have to be distinguished, defined and disclosed separately from the continuing results. Typically in the UK, a layered format is used for the income statement that highlights a number of important components of financial performance:

a)   results from continuing operations (including acquisitions)

b)   results of discontinuing operations

c) profit or loss on the sale or termination of an operation, costs of a fundamental reorganization or restructuring and profits or losses on the disposal of fixed assets

d) extraordinary items (which although defined are effectively prohibited!)

ACCOUNTING POLICIES AND ACCOUNTING ESTIMATES

There is a distinction drawn between accounting policies and accounting estimates. An accounting policy is the basis on which a figure is calculated whereas an accounting estimate is the method by which a figure is calculated. For example – a typical (and required) accounting policy is to depreciate tangible fixed assets. The straight-line and reducing balance methods are two alternative methods of arriving at the figure – the estimate of what the depreciation charge should be.

Key terms

ORDINARY ACTIVITIES

Any activities that are undertaken by a reporting entity as part of its business and such related activities in which the reporting entity engages in furtherance of, incidental to, or arising from these activities.

EXCEPTIONAL OR UNUSUAL ITEMS

Material items that derive from events or transactions that fall within the ordinary activities of the reporting entity for which separate disclosure is required to give the user a proper understanding of the performance of the business.

EXTRAORDINARY ITEMS

Material items possessing a high degree of abnormality that arise from events or transactions that fall outside the ordinary activities of the reporting entity, and that are not expected to recur.

PRIOR PERIOD ADJUSTMENTS

Material adjustments applicable to prior periods arising from changes in accounting policies or from correction of fundamental errors. They do not include normal recurring adjustments or corrections of accounting estimates made in prior periods.

Accounting policies are the specific principles, bases, conventions, rules and practices adopted by an enterprise in preparing and presenting financial statements

TOTAL RECOGNIZED GAINS AND LOSSES

The total of all gains and losses of the reporting entity that are recognized in a period and are attributable to shareholders.

Accounting

DISCLOSURE IN THE INCOME STATEMENT (THIS TOPIC HAS IN A RECENT REVISION OF THE STANDARD BEEN MOVED TO IAS 1)

All items of income and expense should be included in the income statement unless the IAS requires or permits otherwise; e.g. revaluation gains are required to be taken directly to reserves. Although defined and required to be separately disclosed it is considered that **extraordinary items are unlikely to occur**.

The Standard does not define exceptional items but any material 'one-off' income or expense items should be separately disclosed; e.g. settlement of a court case, bankruptcy of a major customer-debtor, restructuring costs.

REVISING ACCOUNTING POLICIES

A change in accounting policy should be made only if required by statute, by an Accounting Standard or if the change will result in a more appropriate presentation of transactions in the financial statement.

DEALING WITH A CHANGE TO ACCOUNTING POLICIES

Figures for the current and previous year should be prepared under the new policy, and opening balances of retained earnings adjusted accordingly. The previous year's comparative figures should also normally be altered.

DEALING WITH A FUNDAMENTAL ERROR

Figures for the current or previous year should be corrected and opening balances of retained earnings adjusted accordingly. The previous year's comparative figures should also normally be altered.

Disclosure

CHANGES TO ACCOUNTING POLICIES AND DEALING WITH FUNDAMENTAL ERRORS

Changes in accounting policies should be disclosed, as should details of any fundamental errors that come to light.

CHANGES IN ACCOUNTING ESTIMATE

If a change in the method of arriving at an accounting estimate currently or in future statements is material then the nature of the change and the amounts involved should be disclosed.

Problem areas and questions to ask about the accounts

REVIEW OF FINAL ACCOUNTS

Questions to ask:

- Is there a full and proper analysis of the components of net profit or loss?

- Are appropriate accounting policies and basis being used?

- Have all material items been disclosed?

- If there are any extraordinary items in the accounts – are they really extraordinary?

NATURE OF THE EVENT AND MATERIALITY OF AMOUNTS

Some events such as disposal of plant and equipment on cessation of one production line may be considered a normal part of business life. Profits or losses on disposals could also be considered merely adjustments to the depreciation charge. Unless truly immaterial, at least less than 10% in amount of net profit or loss, such items should be separately disclosed.

Key differences

Differences between countries tend to be in the 'look' of, and the terminology used, e.g. P&L account (UK) v Income or Revenue statement (US).

As noted above there is a move to introduce a more Standardized and comprehensive statement of total recognized gains and losses.

Objective and definitions from the Standard

Objective

The objective of this Standard is to prescribe the criteria for selecting accounting policies, and the accounting treatment and disclosure of changes in accounting policies, changes in accounting estimates and errors, so that entities prepare and present their financial statements on a consistent basis. This enhances comparability with the entity's financial statements of previous periods and with financial statements of other entities.

Definitions

Accounting policies are the specific principles, bases, conventions, rules and practices adopted by an enterprise in preparing and presenting financial statements.

Errors are omissions from, and other misstatements of, the entity's financial statements for one or more prior periods that are discovered in the current period and relate to reliable information that:

a)   was available when those prior period financial statements were prepared; and

b)   could reasonably be expected to have been obtained and taken into account in the preparation and presentation of those financial statements

Errors include the effects of mathematical mistakes, mistakes in applying accounting policies, oversights or misrepresentations of facts, and fraud.

Extraordinary items are income or expenses that arise from events or transactions that are clearly distinct from the ordinary activities of the enterprise and therefore are not expected to recur frequently or regularly.

Ordinary activities are any activities which are undertaken by an enterprise as part of its business and such related activities in which the enterprise engages in furtherance of, incidental to, or arising from, these activities.

Non-current assets held for sale and discontinued operations – IFRS 5

Why needed

The idea of disclosing discontinued operations (sales, costs, profits or losses) separately from continuing operations has been around for some time (this standard replaces IAS 35 discontinued operations) and makes obvious sense. Such disclosure allows users of accounts to understand the effect of disposal of operations and the sales etc of those parts of the business that will continue.

Without definition of assets held for sale (as a result of disposals) a range of values could be placed on such assets. The standard defines non-current (fixed) assets held for sale.

The drive to have a separate standard, rather than include definitions and accounting in other standards comes from the drive to converge standards. The introduction of the standard specifically mentions this point.

Ideas – concepts

Non-current assets (or groups of such assets – disposal groups) held for sale could be at a going concern 'value' or carrying amount that was considerably in excess of the likely or agreed disposal proceeds. The concept in the standard is that as soon as non-current assets are identified as 'held for sale' then they should be measured at the lower of the carrying amount and fair value less costs to sell. Consequently such non-current assets would no longer be depreciated. Such assets should also be identified separately on the balance sheet.

As is established practice the components of a businesses total profit or loss should be disclosed. That is continuing profits or losses should be distinguished from profits or losses from discontinued transactions (also from one off profits or losses – IAS 8).

Key terms

A non-current asset is an asset that does not meet the definition of a current asset! In simple terms it will be a fixed asset, most likely tangible but also possibly intangible.

Held for sale* means that the assets value or carrying amount will be recovered by selling it rather than through its continuing use in the business.

* What constitutes 'Held for sale' is tightly defined in the standard. The asset (or disposal group) must be available for immediate sale in its present condition subject only to terms that are usual and customary for sales of such assets (or disposal groups) and its sale must be highly probable. Highly probable is further explained.

A discontinued operation is a component of an entity that either has been disposed of or is classified as held for sale and: (a) represents a separate major line of business or geographical area of operations, (b) is part of a single co-ordinated plan to dispose of a separate major line of business or geographical area of operations or (c) is a subsidiary acquired exclusively with a view to resale.

A disposal group is a group of assets to be disposed of, by sale or otherwise, together as a group in a single transaction, and liabilities directly associated with those assets that will be transferred in the transaction. The group includes goodwill acquired in a business combination if the group is a cash-generating unit to which goodwill has been allocated

Accounting

MEASUREMENT OF NON-CURRENT ASSETS (OR DISPOSAL GROUPS) CLASSIFIED AS HELD FOR SALE

An entity shall measure a non-current asset (or disposal group) classified as held for sale at the lower of its carrying amount and fair value less costs to sell. An entity shall recognise an impairment loss for any initial or subsequent write-down of the asset (or disposal group) and an entity shall recognise a gain for any subsequent increase in fair value less costs to sell of an asset, but not in excess of the cumulative impairment loss that has been recognised

Disclosure

CLASSIFICATION OF NON-CURRENT ASSETS (OR DISPOSAL GROUPS) AS HELD FOR SALE

An entity shall classify a non-current asset (or disposal group) as held for sale if its carrying amount will be recovered principally through a sale transaction rather than through continuing use. An entity shall present a non-current asset classified as held for sale and the assets of a disposal group classified as held for sale separately from other assets in the balance sheet.

Non-current assets that are to be abandoned should not be classed as held for sale as carrying value may be recovered from continuing use – till time of abandonment. If abandoned activities form a material component of an entity then they should be disclosed separately.

If a plan to sell and asset is terminated then the asset will cease to be classified as 'held for sale' and the asset reinstated as a non-current asset and accounted for if it had continued in use.

DETAILS OF DISCONTINUED OPERATIONS (AND DISPOSAL OF NON-CURRENT ASSETS)

An entity shall present and disclose information that enables users of the financial statements to evaluate the financial effects of discontinued operations and disposals of non-current assets (or disposal groups). Paragraphs 31 to 36 and 41 and 42 give details of information that should be disclosed.

Objective

The objective of this IFRS is to specify the accounting for assets held for sale, and the presentation and disclosure of *discontinued operations*. In particular, the IFRS requires:

a) assets that meet the criteria to be classified as held for sale to be measured at the lower of carrying amount and fair value less costs to sell, and depreciation on such assets to cease; and

b) assets that meet the criteria to be classified as held for sale to be presented separately on the face of the balance sheet and the results of discontinued operations to be presented separately in the income statement

Definitions

A cash-generating unit is the smallest identifiable group of assets that generates cash inflows that are largely independent of the cash inflows from other assets or groups of assets.

Component of an entity are operations and cash flows that can be clearly distinguished, operationally and for financial reporting purposes, from the rest of the entity.

Costs to sell are the incremental costs directly attributable to the disposal of an asset (or disposal group), excluding finance costs and income tax expense.

Current assets are an asset that satisfies any of the following criteria:

a) it is expected to be realised in, or is intended for sale or consumption in, the entity's normal operating cycle;

b) it is held primarily for the purpose of being traded;

c) it is expected to be realised within twelve months after the balance sheet date; or

d) it is cash or a cash equivalent asset unless it is restricted from being exchanged or used to settle a liability for at least twelve months after the balance sheet date.

A discontinued operation is a component of an entity that either has been disposed of or is classified as held for sale and: (a) represents a separate major line of business or geographical area of operations, (b) is part of a single co-ordinated plan to dispose of a separate major line of business or geographical area of operations or (c) is a subsidiary acquired exclusively with a view to resale.

A disposal group is a group of assets to be disposed of, by sale or otherwise, together as a group in a single transaction, and liabilities directly associated with those assets that will be transferred in the transaction. The group includes goodwill acquired in a business combination if the group is a cash-generating unit to which goodwill has been allocated in accordance with the requirements of paragraphs 80-87 of IAS 36 *Impairment of Assets* (as revised in 2004) or if it is an operation within such a cash-generating unit.

Fair value is the amount for which an asset could be exchanged, or a liability settled, between knowledgeable, willing parties in an arm's length transaction.

A firm purchase commitment is an agreement with an unrelated party, binding on both parties and usually legally enforceable, that:

a) specifies all significant terms, including the price and timing of the transactions, and

b) includes a disincentive for non-performance that is sufficiently large to make performance highly probable.

Highly probable is significantly more likely than probable.

A non-current asset is an asset that does not meet the definition of a current asset.

Probable means more likely than not.

Recoverable amount is the higher of an asset's fair value less costs to sell and its value in use.

Value in use is the present value of estimated future cash flows expected to arise from the continuing use of an asset and from its disposal at the end of its useful life.

First time adoption of international accounting standards – IFRS 1

Why needed

International Accounting Standards are different from the UK Standards. Some industry results will be much more affected than others. The main thrust of this first IFRS is that adoption should not be impossible because of the time or cost required in dealing with every nuance of the Standards.

Ideas – concepts

Standards should be complied with – but the introduction should not be hindered by undue expense or time required for compliance.

Accounting

The starting point for accounting under IFRS's is an opening IFRS balance sheet at the date of transition to IFRS's.

An entity shall use the same accounting policies in its opening IFRS balance sheet and throughout all periods presented in its first IFRS financial statements. Those accounting policies shall comply with each IFRS effective at the reporting date for its first IFRS financial statements.

An entity may use one or more of the exemptions listed and explained in the IFRS:

- business combinations
- fair value or revaluation as deemed cost
- employee benefits
- cumulative translation differences
- compound financial instruments
- assets and liabilities of subsidiaries, associates and joint ventures.

There are exceptions to retrospective application of some IFRS's:

- de-recognition of financial assets and financial liabilities
- hedge accounting
- estimates

Disclosure

To comply with IAS 1 Presentation of Financial Statements, an entity's first IFRS financial statements shall include at least one year of comparative information under IFRS's.

An entity shall explain how the transition, from previous GAAP to IFRS's affects its financial position, financial performance and cash flows.

Problem areas and questions to ask about the accounts

THE TIME NEEDED

Even for a straightforward business there is a lot of work to do. The first year is not 2005 for relevant EU companies but 2004 or even earlier if reliable comparatives are to be given.

Objective and definitions from the Standard

Objective

An entity shall apply this IFRS in:

a) its first IFRS financial statements; and

b) each interim financial report, if any, that it presents under IAS 34 Interim Financial Reporting for part of the period covered by its first IFRS financial statements.

Definitions

Date of transition to IFRS's is the beginning of the earliest period for which an entity presents full comparative information under IFRS's in its first full IFRS statements.

First IFRS financial statements are the first annual financial statements in which an entity adopts IFRS's, by an explicit and unreserved statement of compliance with IFRS's.

A **first time adopter** is an entity that presents its first IFRS financial statements.

IFRS's are Standards and Interpretations adopted by the International Accounting Standards Board (IASB). They comprise:

a) International Financial reporting Standards

b) International Accounting Standards

c) Interpretations originated by the International Financial Reporting Interpretations Committee (IFRIC) or former Standing Interpretations Committee (SIC), and adopted by the IASB

An **opening IFRS balance sheet** is an entity's balance sheet (published or unpublished) at the date of transition to IFRS's.

Previous GAAP is the basis of accounting that a first-time adopter used immediately before adopting IFRS's.

The reporting date is the end of the latest period covered by financial statements or by an interim financial report.

Cash flow statements – IAS 7

Why needed

Positive cash flow is essential for the survival and growth of any business.

The balance sheet can tell you where you are, the income statement can tell you what income and expenditure there was (these include accrued amounts), but only a cash flow statement can tell you what, if any, cash is being generated, how it is being sourced and how it's used.

Identifying how cash has flown through a business is very useful in verifying a businesses performance for a period and movement in net asset position over a period.

After the debacle of Worldcom, Enron etc. credit analysts woke up to the fact that maybe they had not been doing their job. On quizzing the CEO of a reputable company about whether reported profits were real he replied 'lift the hatch and the dollars are there' – a good retort!

Ideas – concepts

The majority of business transactions are cash based, that is cash, or more likely bank account, receipts and payments are involved. Thus a statement could be prepared listing cash in and cash out, grouped into:

- Cash in and out from trading, from **operating activities**.
- Cash out into investments or fixed assets, or in from the sale of the same – **investing activities**.
- Cash in from raising new equity or loans, or out from the reduction in loans or equity – **financing activities**.

These headings cover all the activities that a business can get involved in and the net cash in or out will be the change in the net cash position* over the period.

*(Cash on hand, deposited at a bank or overdraft.)

A cash flow statement simply groups cash flows as follows:

- **Cash flows from operating activities.**
- **Cash flows from investing activities.**
- **Cash flows from financing activities.**
- **Net increase (/decrease) in cash and cash equivalents.**

The cash flow statement could be prepared from the cash book and bank accounts. This would show gross receipts from customers, payments to suppliers and employees, payments for the purchase of fixed assets and proceeds of long-term borrowings etc. This would reveal the basic cash flows by type and is called the **direct method**. This is the method preferred by the Standard, but rarely followed. The drawbacks are that there is no clear reconciliation with operating profit and detailed cash and bank analysis has to be done.

The **indirect method** arrives at the cash flow headings above by starting with operating profit which has non-cash figures (e.g. accruals and depreciation) along with movements in working capital (e.g. money tied up in stock) added back to give the operating cash flow. There is thus reconciliation between operating profit reported in the income statement and operating cash flow. This can be shown on the face of the cash flow statement or as a note.

The investing and financing cash flows can be identified by analyzing the movement in balance sheet figures, e.g. fixed assets additions are an investing cash out flow.

Cash flow statements are in essence simple to prepare using the indirect method. For a successful company this would mean the movement in cash and bank balances can be explained by cash inflows from operation of the business, less outflows on investment plus inflows from funding through loans or equity.

There is an example of the layout and preparation of a cash flow statement in chapter 1.1.

Key terms

Cash comprises cash on hand and demand deposits less overdrafts.

Cash equivalents are short-term, highly liquid investments that are readily convertible into cash.

Operating activities are the principal trading revenue producing activities of the enterprise.

Investing activities are the acquisition and disposal of long-term assets (tangible and intangible fixed assets and investments).

Financing activities are activities that result in changes in shareholders' equity and funding (increases in share capital, increases or decreases in loans).

Accounting

An enterprise should report cash flows from operating activities using either:

a) the direct method where major classes of gross cash receipts and payments are disclosed; or

b) the indirect method where the net profit or loss for the period is adjusted for the effect of non-cash transactions (items are 'un' or 'dis' accrued and depreciation, never a cash cost, is added back).

Disclosure

The cash flow statement should report cash flows during the period classified by operating, investing and financing activities.

A breakdown of individual types of items should be given under the above headings. In particular, cash flows related to taxation should be separately disclosed under one or more of the three headings.

Problem areas and questions to ask about the accounts

RECONCILING INCOME STATEMENT AND BALANCE SHEET FIGURES – EXPLAINING THE CASH AND DEBT MOVEMENTS

It is in the area of reconciling and explaining movements in cash, bank deposits and overdrafts that both the Standard and practice are often far from clear. The information will be given but the reader of the accounts has to study the statements and, particularly, the notes very carefully.

SIGNIFICANT DIFFERENCES IN GAAP

The existing UK Standard (FRS1) requires up to 9 headings (management of liquid resources and financing may be combined).

These are cash flows related to:

- operating activities

- dividends from joint ventures and associates

- returns on investments and servicing of finance

- taxation

- capital expenditure and financial investment

- acquisitions and disposals

- equity dividends paid

- management of liquid resources

- financing

The final figure on the cash flow statement is then reconciled to movement in net debt – a note on analysis of changes in net debt may also be needed. These are not part of the cash flow statement! This supports the point made under explaining cash and debt movement, that identifying just where the cash came from, or went to, can be difficult. Many companies reporting is poor in this respect.

WHAT IS CASH?

The definition of cash in the UK Standard is particularly tight, less so in the IAS.

Objective and definitions from the Standard

Objective

Information about cash flows of an enterprise is useful in providing users of financial statements with a basis to assess the ability of the enterprise to generate cash and cash equivalents, and the needs of the enterprise to utilize those cash flows. The economic decisions that are taken by users require an evaluation of the ability of an enterprise to generate cash and cash equivalents, and the timing and certainty of their generation.

The objective of this Standard is to require the provision of information about historical changes in cash and cash equivalents of an enterprise by means of a cash flow statement which classifies cash flows during the period from operating, investing and financing activities.

Definitions

Cash comprises cash on hand and demand deposits.

Cash equivalents are short-term, highly liquid investments that are readily convertible to known amounts of cash and which are subject to an insignificant risk of changes in value.

Cash flows are inflows and out flows of cash and cash equivalents.

Operating activities are the principal revenue producing activities of the enterprise and other activities that are not investing or financing activities.

Investing activities are the acquisition and disposal of long-term assets and other investments not included in cash equivalents.

Financing activities are activities that result in changes in the size and composition of the equity capital and borrowings of the enterprise.

Interim financial reporting – IAS 34

Why needed

Listed companies, as a matter of good governance and because of stock market listing requirements will report half yearly and even quarterly. This Standard is another where the other demands for reporting and disclosure would seem to make the need for a Standard superfluous.

Ideas – concepts

Interim financial statements should contain the same individual reports and use the same accounting policies as the annual statutory accounts. It may be acceptable and practical to demand less detail in some of the disclosures and notes.

Key terms

Interim financial report means a financial report containing either a complete set of financial statements (as described in IAS1 – Presentation of Financial Statements) or a set of condensed financial statements (as described in this Standard) for an interim period.

Accounting

The only accounting issue is that more figures may be based on estimates.

Disclosure

MINIMUM REQUIREMENTS

a)   a condensed balance sheet

b)   a condensed income statement

c)   a condensed cash flow statement

d)   a condensed statement of changes in equity

e)   selected explanatory notes

The Standard does give examples of what might be in condensed financial statements, but it is far more likely that relevant company law or stock market listing rules will dictate what is disclosed. This is likely to be more than the Standard demands.

Problem areas and questions to ask about the accounts

THE USE OF ESTIMATES

Estimates have to be made when preparing financial statements. For some types of business this can involve much work both for the statement preparers and auditors. When producing interim accounts (possibly to tight deadlines) the level of effort, and thus accuracy of estimates, may be (acceptably) less.

If an estimate used at the interim stage has to be changed significantly when the full annual statements are produced, that fact should be disclosed.

MATERIALITY

The level of 'what is material' should be reviewed. Whilst there may be more estimates used materiality still has to be considered in relation to level of profits etc.

Objective and definitions from the Standard

Objective

The objective of this Standard is to prescribe the minimum content of an interim financial report, and to prescribe the principles for recognition and measurement in complete or condensed statements, for an interim period. Timely and reliable interim financial reporting improves the ability of investors, creditors and others to understand an enterprises' capacity to generate earnings and cash flows and its financial condition and liquidity.

Definitions

An interim period is a financial reporting period shorter than a full financial year.

An interim financial report means a financial report containing either a complete set of financial statements (as described in IAS1 – Presentation of Financial Statements) or a set of condensed financial statements (as described in this Standard) for an interim period.

THREE

Accounting methods and conventions

3.1

Property, plant and equipment – IAS 16

Why needed

Property, plant and equipment or tangible fixed assets are frequently major assets and thus components of capital employed in businesses. Stating how they are valued is essential to an understanding of balance sheet worth.

Another related issue is whether tangible fixed assets are real. Worldcom was a good example of a business capitalizing costs – treating operating costs as fixed assets, thus reducing costs, increasing profits and increasing balance sheet 'worth'!

Ideas – concepts

The principal issue with tangible fixed assets is – at what value are they stated in the balance sheet? Also is the cost of use or loss in value, of the asset fairly reported in the profit and loss account? The following are specific value related issues.

Tangible fixed assets have to be shown in a balance sheet, but at what value? 'Value' could mean cost, a written down value or a revalued amount. The simplest approach is to record them at what they originally cost, thereafter reducing the cost by charging a deduction for consumption as they are consumed in generating profits – as they depreciate with use.

Tangible fixed assets such as property frequently appreciate in value. They should best be shown at revalued amount.

Assets can cease to hold value. For example, specialized equipment in a business making products for which there is a sudden, permanent lack of demand. The value of this plant and equipment has been impaired and thus the asset value should be written down to a recoverable amount, if any.

Profits or losses on disposal or impairment of fixed assets occur in the normal course of business, but are often large in amount and should be reported separately.

Key terms

Property, plant and equipment are tangible assets that are held by an enterprise for use, for rental to others or for administrative purposes; and are expected to be used during more than one period.

Depreciation is the systematic allocation of the cost or other substituted amount of an asset over its useful life.

Impairment is a reduction in the recoverable amount of a fixed asset or goodwill below its carrying amount – see IAS 36 for further definition and guidance.

Accounting

Value – An item of property, plant or equipment should be carried at cost, or at a revalued amount, but less any accumulated depreciation or impairment write down.

Depreciation – should be allocated on a systematic basis over the assets life and recognized as an expense.

Disclosure

Details of the measurement basis, the depreciation method with the expected asset lives or rate of depreciation for each class of asset.

A reconciliation of the carrying amount in the balance sheet from the start to finish of the year. This should show all the components of movement, e.g. purchases, disposals, depreciation or impairment write downs.

Problem areas and questions to ask about your accounts

Valuation basis – On what basis are our tangible fixed assets valued? When was the last valuation and how frequently are they carried out? Who carried out the valuation – are they independent?

Costs – are the costs of the assets genuine? This is a particular problem with 'own build' fixed assets. The questions to ask are 'are they arms length costs?' and 'do the costs hold value?'

Useful lives residual values and depreciation methods – Should be reviewed annually as being realistic and appropriate.

Impairment – Has an impairment review been carried out? That is are there any indications that the tangibles fixed assets are seriously overvalued and their value will not be recovered from continued profitable use?

Finance costs – Have finance costs been capitalized? Where an entity adopts a policy of capitalizing finance costs, finance costs that are directly attributable to the construction of tangible fixed assets should be capitalized as part of the cost of those assets – see IAS 23 Borrowing Costs.

Accounting for repairs and maintenance – Subsequent expenditure to ensure that the tangible fixed asset maintains its previously assessed standard of performance should be recognized in the profit and loss account as it is incurred.

Subsequent expenditure should be capitalized when the costs give probable economic benefits in excess of the original (economic benefits). That is there is a genuine enhancement of the asset's performance or life.

In the UK Standard the following specific conditions have to be met:

a) where the subsequent expenditure provides an enhancement of the economic benefits of the tangible asset in excess of the previously assessed Standard of performance.

b) where a component of the tangible fixed asset that has been treated separately for depreciation purposes and depreciated over its individual economic life, is replaced or restored.

c) where the subsequent expenditure relates to a major inspection or overhaul of a tangible fixed asset that restores the economic benefits of the asset that have been consumed by the entity and have already been reflected in depreciation.

Key differences

In the UK Standard (FRS15) there is finessing on what current value means. The current value of a tangible fixed asset to the business is the lower of replacement costs and recoverable amount. FRS15 then goes on to finesse on what recoverable amount is. The UK Standard requires that the following valuation basis should be used for revalued properties that are not impaired:

a) non specialized properties should be valued on the basis of existing use (EUV)

b) specialized properties should be valued on the basis of depreciated replacement cost

c) properties surplus to an entity's requirements should be valued on the basis of open market value (OMV)

Tangible fixed assets other than properties should be valued using market value, where possible. Where market value is not obtainable, assets should be valued on the basis of depreciated replacement cost.

Objective and definitions used in the Standard

Objective

The objective of this Standard is to prescribe the accounting treatment for property, plant and equipment. The principal issues in accounting for property, plant and equipment are the timing of recognition of the assets, the determination of their carrying amounts and the depreciation charges to be recognized in relation to them.

This Standard requires an item of property, plant and equipment to be recognized as an asset when it satisfies the definition and recognition criteria for an asset in the Framework, for the preparation and Presentation of Financial Statements.

More specific objectives can be found in the UK FRS, these are that:

a) consistent principles are applied to the initial measurement of tangible fixed assets.

b) where an entity chooses to revalue tangible fixed assets the valuation is performed on a consistent basis and kept up to date, and gains and losses on re-valuation are recognized on a consistent basis.

c) depreciation of tangible fixed assets is calculated in a consistent manner and recognized as the economic benefits are consumed over the assets' useful economic lives.

d) sufficient information is disclosed in the financial statements to enable users to understand the impact of the entity's accounting policies regarding initial measurement, valuation and depreciation of tangible fixed assets on the financial position and performance of the entity.

Property, plant and equipment are tangible assets that:

a) are held by an entity for use in the production or supply of goods or services, for rental to others, or for administrative purposes; and

b) are expected to be used during more than one period.

A depreciable amount is the cost of an asset or other amount substituted for cost in the financial statements, less its residual value.

Depreciation is the systematic allocation of the depreciable amount of an asset over its useful life.

Useful life is either:

a) the period of time over which an asset is expected to be used by the entity; or

b) the number of production or similar units expected to be obtained from the asset by the entity.

Cost is the amount of cash or cash equivalents paid, or the fair value of the other consideration given to acquire an asset at the time of its acquisition or construction.

Residual value of an asset is the estimated amount that the entity would currently obtain from disposal of the asset, after deducting the estimated costs of disposal, if the asset were already of the age and in the condition expected at the end of its useful life.

Fair value is the amount for which an asset could be exchanged between knowledgeable, willing parties in an arm's length transaction.

Carrying amount is the amount at which an asset is recognized after deducting any accumulated depreciation and accumulated impairment losses.

Impairment loss is the amount by which the carrying amount of an asset exceeds its recoverable amount.

3.2

Investment property – IAS 40

Why needed

Fixed assets are generally subject to depreciation charges to reflect on a systematic basis the wearing out, consumption or other loss of value. A different treatment is required where a significant proportion of fixed assets are held not for consumption but as investments. The current value and changes in that value are of prime importance.

Ideas – concepts

Investment properties are held for gain in value – they are not 'consumable' assets and therefore should not be depreciated.

Key terms

INVESTMENT PROPERTY

An investment property is an investment in land or buildings:

a) in respect of which construction work and development have been completed; and

b) which is held for its investment potential, any rental income being negotiated at arm's length.

Own or group occupied buildings cannot be classified as investment properties in group accounts, but may be treated as Investment properties in the individual company's accounts.

Accounting

INITIAL MEASUREMENT

An investment property should be initially recorded at its cost including any transaction costs. Transaction costs are considered to be directly attributable costs such as legal fees, property transfer taxes etc. Subsequent expenditure on the property should be recognized as an expense unless the expenditure enhances the value of the property, e.g. through the ability to charge higher rents.

MEASUREMENT IN SUBSEQUENT ACCOUNTING PERIODS

Under the fair value model an investment property should be revalued to fair value at the balance sheet date, where fair value reflects the actual state and circumstances as at the balance sheet date. Any gain or loss arising from a change in fair value should be included in the profit or loss for the period.

If the benchmark treatment of valuing investment properties at fair value is followed then that method should apply to **all** investment properties. Exceptions are if the allowed alternative treatment of valuing property at cost* is followed or (exceptionally) if no fair value can be determined on a continuing basis.

* Properties are stated at original (historical) cost less accumulated depreciation or impairment.

Disclosure

The methods and significant assumption (if any) applied in determining the fair value of investment property. If classification is difficult the criteria developed to distinguish owner occupied and investment property.

The extent to which fair value of an investment property is based on a valuation by an independent valuer who holds a relevant and recognized professional qualification.

A reconciliation of the carrying amount of the investment property at the beginning of the accounting period through to the balance sheet date.

Amounts included in the income statement arising from rental income and related direct operating costs. Any direct operating costs related to investment property from which no rental income arises should also be disclosed:

Any restrictions (with amount) on the realizability of the investment property and any material contractual obligations related to investment properties.

If the benchmark treatment is not used then an explanation should be given as to why not, along with details as for tangible fixed assets under IAS 16 Property Plant and Equipment.

Problem areas and questions to ask about the accounts

CLASSIFICATION OF PROPERTIES AND TRANSFERS

There may be cases where a view could be taken as to whether a property is held as an investment or not. Also changes from owner occupancy (particularly temporary partial occupancy) could cause uncertainty about classification. The definitions in the Standard should help.

TREATMENT OF CHANGES IN INVESTMENT PROPERTY VALUES

The requirement that any gain or loss arising from a change in the fair value should be included in net profit or loss for the period raises the issue of exactly where in the income statement such changes should be disclosed. They represent unrealized gains or losses being recognized in the income statement.

It should be noted that the requirement – the benchmark treatment – to revalue investment properties to fair value, is an example of the true and fair override and departure from the normal practice, under the UK Companies Act, which requires depreciation of fixed assets that have a limited useful life.

FAIR VALUE OR THE COST MODEL

Which do the directors believe gives the most relevant information? Most would say the fair value model is better.

Key differences

In the UK if the person carrying out the valuation is an employee of the company then that fact should be stated. Also, in the UK, changes in fair value (except when there is a fall in value below historic cost) are taken to reserves and reported through the statement of Total Recognized Gains and Losses.

Objective and definitions from the Standard

Objective

The objective of this Standard is to prescribe the accounting treatment for investment property and related disclosure requirements.

Definitions

Investment property is property (land or building – or part of a building – or both) held to earn rentals or for capital appreciation or both, rather than for:

a) use in the productive supply of goods or services or for administration purposes; or

b) sale in the ordinary course of business.

A property interest that is held by a lessee under an operating lease may be classified as investment property if and only if, in addition to the above condition being met, the lessee uses the fair value model set out in paragraphs 27-49 of the Standard. A lessee that uses the cost model set out in the Standard shall not classify property held under an operating lease as investment property.

Owner occupied property is property held (by the owner or by the lessee under a finance lease) for use in the production or supply of goods or services, or for administrative purposes.

Fair value is the amount for which an asset could be exchanged between knowledgeable, willing parties in an arm's length transaction.

Cost is the amount of cash or cash equivalents paid, or the fair value of the other consideration given to acquire an asset at the time of its acquisition or construction.

Carrying amount is the amount at which an asset is recognized in the balance sheet.

3.3
Inventories – IAS 2

Why needed

Over (or under) valuing inventory (stock) affects the balance sheet asset value. BUT the valuation also affects the related cost of sales, and thus profit by the same amount. If one wanted to manipulate profit then stock valuation would be an obvious choice.

Inventories (stocks) are so critical to the reporting of profits or losses at the correct amount, in the correct period, that clear definition of terms and defined accounting is required. The costs to be included, the condition, sale ability, and thus value of stocks, will often be subjective. There is ample scope for errors or manipulation of figures!

Ideas – concepts

The basic concept is that stock should be included in accounts at cost (what was paid for them) or a lower figure, net realizable value, if they are now worth less.

The exercise of counting or taking stock at the end of an accounting period is the **matching** concept in action. A simple example of the arithmetic of the stock adjustment is shown below.

- materials purchased in the period   8,500
- stock held at the end of the period   800
- therefore materials sold or taken
  into production in the period   7,700

A question arises over what figure to use for the value of stock. In the simple example above, the conventional and normally correct figure is the cost of the remaining stock. Stock or WIP should be valued at what it cost.

However, if for some reason the stock on hand had deteriorated, or could be replaced at a (permanently) much lower price, then the stock should be written down to its net realizable value (nrv). This is the **prudence** concept in operation.

Much can be made of what is the cost of stock or WIP. If stock items are purchased piecemeal over time then what is the cost of the stock at the period end? In the UK it is generally accepted that stock should be accounted for and therefore valued on a 'first in first out basis'-FIFO, that is remaining stock is assumed to be the most recently purchased. This seems entirely reasonable as stock will be at an up to date cost. Also it is likely that the oldest stock will be sold first.

Key terms

COST

The cost of inventories should comprise all costs of purchase, costs of conversion and other costs incurred in bringing the inventories to their present location and condition.

NET REALIZABLE VALUE

The estimated selling price in the ordinary course of business, less the estimated costs of completion and the estimated costs necessary to make the sale.

Accounting

Inventories should be measured at the lower of cost or net realizable value.

Costs should ideally be assigned to each item of inventory on a FIFO (first in first out basis). In practice an approximation for individually costing each item is acceptable, e.g. a supermarket can more easily count and value inventories at the retail selling price; the supermarket will very accurately know the VAT (sales tax) element and the mark up from cost, and can thus reduce inventories valued at retail to a very reliable approximation of the cost.

At all times business must look out for slow moving, obsolete or damaged inventories which will not sell at cost, or at all. Any such items should be written down to their net realizable value.

Disclosure

Financial statements should disclose:

- the accounting policies adopted in measuring inventories.

- the amounts of inventories at cost or net realizable value appropriately classified. In the UK the minimum classifications are: raw materials, work-in-progress and finished goods.

- details and amounts of any reversal of previous inventory write downs.

- the value of any inventories pledged as security for liabilities.

Problem areas and questions to ask about the accounts

STOCK FRAUD AND ERROR

The counting of stock as well as valuing it is often prone to error or deliberate manipulation. Proper controls over stock and stock-taking are essential. Analytical review of margins, amounts of stock, stock movements etc., can be an effective way of identifying wrong figures.

BASIS OF STOCK VALUATION

What basis has been used to value stock? What costs have been included in stock? Do all costs genuinely relate to getting stock to its current location and position? Have all obsolete, damaged and out of date stock items been identified and written down to net realizable value?

STOCK WRITE-DOWNS

As inventories or stock and short-term work-in-progress are often material assets whose valuation directly affects reported profit or loss, a clear understanding of the stock-taking and valuation procedures is essential. If stock write downs are to be made then the basis of, and thus adequacy of, the write-down should be understood.

Key differences

The US generally uses the LIFO basis for valuing inventories. This leads to a lower value of inventories. A revision to the Standard will not allow FIFO as an alternative treatment.

Objective and definitions from the Standard

Objective

The objective of this Standard is to prescribe the accounting treatment for inventories. A primary issue in accounting for inventories is the amount of cost to be recognized as an asset and carried forward until related revenues are recognized. This Standard provides guidance on the determination of cost and its subsequent recognition as an expense, including any write downs to net realizable value. It also provides guidance on the cost formulas that are used to assign costs to inventories.

Definitions

Inventories are assets:

a) held for sale in the ordinary course of business;

b) in the process of production for such sale; or

c) in the form of materials or supplies to be consumed in the production process or in the rendering of services.

COST

The cost of inventories should comprise all costs of purchase, costs of conversion and other costs incurred in bringing the inventories to their present location and condition.

NET REALIZABLE VALUE

This is the estimated selling price in the ordinary course of business, less the estimated costs of completion and the estimated costs necessary to make the sale.

COST OF PURCHASE

The cost of purchase comprises purchase price including import duties, transport and handling costs and any other directly attributable costs, less trade discounts, rebates and subsidies.

COST OF CONVERSION

The cost of conversion comprises:

* costs that are specifically attributable to units of production; and

* production overheads and other overheads, if they are attributable to bringing the product or service to its present location and condition.

PRODUCTION OVERHEADS

Overheads incurred in respect of materials, labor or services for production, based on the normal level of activity.

OTHER COSTS

Other costs are included in the cost of inventories only to the extent that they are incurred in bringing the inventories to their present location and condition, e.g. costs of designing products for specific customers.

COST OF INVENTORIES OF A SERVICE PROVIDER

The cost of inventories of a service provider consists primarily of the labour and other costs of personnel directly engaged in providing the service, including supervisory personnel and attributable overheads. Labour and other costs relating to sales and general administrative personnel are not included, but are recognized as expenses in the period in which they are incurred.

Intangible assets – IAS 38

Why needed

For many businesses the principal assets they own and employ in business are 'intangible' fixed assets, that is, they are long-term assets with lives of more than 12 months. They are the 'infrastructure' on which, and by which, the business earns its future cash flows and profits. One meaning of intangible is 'not cognizable by the sense of touch' this implies that they cannot be touched but the meaning implied by accountants is more realistically interpreted as 'difficult to value'. Intangibles such as patents, brands, know-how and, in general terms, goodwill are difficult to value. A prudent treatment would be to write off the intangible as soon as it was purchased. This write-off would be done across the balance sheet, against retained profits or reserves. Whilst prudent, this has the effect of understating the capital employed in the business.

Unless the premium paid for goodwill really was for a worthless asset then there would be some future enhanced earnings arising out of the goodwill – these would show up in subsequent earnings figures.

A fairer presentation is considered to be to show the goodwill as an asset (thus part of capital employed). This intangible fixed asset should then be charged to the profit and loss account over the period for which enhanced earnings arise – the matching concept.

Ideas – concepts

Intangible things are difficult to comprehend – the second meaning in the Oxford English Dictionary is 'That cannot be grasped mentally'! Thus premia paid for goodwill and its constituents, a name, brands, patents, know-how etc., may be difficult to value. However, money has been paid and the value at date of acquisition is presumably a fair value. But what is fair? If several companies are chasing a 'must have' business then rational fairness goes out the window!

Purchased intangibles are part of the capital employed of a business and should be shown at cost in the balance sheet. At present the view is taken that intangibles should be written off over a period of 20 years maximum, or less if the intangible has a shorter life, e.g. a license that expires after 7 years would be written off over 7 years. If it can be demonstrated that the intangible's value, e.g. a brand name, is supported by expense on promotion etc., then the intangible can remain in the balance sheet at cost. The exercise of checking whether the intangible holds value is carried out as an 'impairment' review (see IAS 36 -Impairment of Assets). The argument is that the promotion costs etc., are the matched costs to be deducted from income – the intangible retains its value.

There has been much debate about the period over which intangibles should be written off and 5, 10, 20 or whatever years are all probably arbitrary. A revision of the Standard will take the view that intangibles should be shown at cost, but subject to annual impairment reviews. This revision omits to deal with the question of revaluing intangibles and own generated intangibles – see Problem Areas overleaf.

Key terms

An **intangible asset** is an identifiable non-monetary asset without physical substance held for use in the production or supply of goods or services, for rental to others, or for administrative purposes. This is the definition from the Standard, but not a very good one. Many intangibles do have physical substance – e.g. patents and related drawings, and license agreements – the issue really is that intangibles are difficult to value.

Impairment loss is the amount by which the carrying amount of an asset exceeds its recoverable amount.

Accounting

An intangible asset should only be recognized (in the balance sheet) if it is probable that future economic benefits will flow to the enterprise as a result of owing the asset **and** the cost of the asset can be measured reliably. Otherwise, expenditure on an intangible item should be recognized as an expense when it is incurred.

The Standard has many more definitions and twists to its logic but in the end it demands that only purchased goodwill or intangible assets can be shown in the balance sheet. Internally generated goodwill or assets (e.g. a new brand) cannot be capitalized and shown in the balance sheet. The argument is that it will inevitably be impossible to measure the cost reliably.

Intangibles that are permitted to be capitalized should then be written off – amortized over a prudent period or carried at cost if they can demonstrably be shown to hold value – an annual impairment review should be carried out.

Research costs should be written off as incurred, the argument being that at the stage of research it is too difficult to identify and measure the probable future economic benefits that may flow from the research.

Development costs may be capitalized but only if they meet very strict criteria:

- they are clearly identifiable and measurable;
- they relate to a technically viable project;
- the development costs are likely to be recovered – the project is likely to be commercially viable; and
- the organization has the funding to complete the development.

Disclosure

Financial statements should disclose for each distinct class of intangible asset:

a) the useful life, amortisation rate and method.
b) the gross carrying amount and accumulated amortisation at the beginning and end of the period.

Problem areas and questions to ask about the accounts

All intangible worth related to goodwill, brands and other intangible fixed assets whether purchased or internally generated, could be shown as intangible fixed assets (at fair cost/value). This would reveal what the directors of a company had invested in capital employed. This could then be written off and thus matched with the enhanced revenue streams generated (or not!).

For internally generated goodwill and intangible fixed assets, the Standard shies away from this approach – presumably as valuation of intangibles is too subjective. BUT if the approach and arithmetic of IAS 36 – Impairment of Assets can be used to identify falling intangible value, could the same techniques not be used to support intangible valuation? The answer to this is that the Standard setters refute that it is possible to measure the cost reliably. It is suggested that companies with material own generated goodwill, and other intangibles, declare these and give indications of their value in a Financial Review included in the financial statements.

Companies that have developed, own and have enhanced brand or other intangibles values are generally aware of their worth and can, and do, consider their values in internal management accounts. Being aware of the return that is made on brands is a very important issue for many businesses.

Key differences

There have been many different treatments of goodwill and other intangibles in different countries over the years, but harmonisation means that only purchased goodwill and other intangibles may be capitalized at their purchase cost. This cost will then be subject to annual impairment review.

Objective and definitions from the Standard

Objective

The objective of this Standard is to prescribe the accounting treatment for intangible fixed assets that are not dealt with in another International Accounting Standard. This Standard requires an enterprise to recognize an intangible asset if, and only if, certain criteria are met. The Standard also specifies how to measure the carrying amount of intangible assets and requires certain disclosures about them.

Definitions

An **intangible asset** is an identifiable non-monetary asset without physical substance held for use in the production or supply of goods or services, for rental to others, or for administrative purposes.

An **asset** is a resource:

a) controlled by an enterprise as a result of past events; and

b) from which future economic benefits are expected to flow to the enterprise.

Monetary assets are monies held and assets to be received in fixed or determinable amounts of money.

Research is original and planned investigation undertaken with the prospect of gaining new scientific or technical knowledge and understanding.

Development is the application of research findings or other knowledge to a plan or design for the production of new or substantially improved materials, devices, products, processes, systems or services, prior to the commencement of commercial production or use.

Amortization is the systematic allocation of the depreciable amount of an intangible asset over its useful life.

Depreciable amount is the cost of an asset, or other amount substituted for cost in the financial statements, less its residual value.

Useful life is either:

a) the period of time over which an asset is expected to be used by the enterprise; or

b) the number of production or similar units expected to be obtained from the asset by the enterprise.

Cost is the amount of cash or cash equivalents paid, or the fair value of the other consideration given to acquire an asset at the time of its acquisition or production.

Residual value is the net amount which an enterprise expects to obtain for an asset at the end of its useful life, after deducting the expected costs of disposal.

Fair value of an asset is the amount for which that asset could be exchanged between knowledgeable, willing parties in an arm's length transaction.

An **active market** is a market where all the following conditions exist:

a) the items traded within the market are homogeneous;

b) willing buyers and sellers can normally be found at any time; and

c) prices are available to the public.

Carrying amount is the amount at which an asset is recognized in the balance sheet after deducting any accumulated amortization and accumulated impairment losses thereon.

Impairment loss is the amount by which the carrying amount of an asset exceeds its recoverable amount.

Impairment of fixed assets – IAS 36

Why needed

With the requirement to include goodwill and other intangibles as assets in the balance sheet there is a need to have some 'science' as to how these are valued, particularly as by nature their value is 'intangible'. This Standard aims to provide the framework for prudently valuing goodwill, intangibles and also tangible fixed assets.

Ideas – concepts

After acquisition the net book amount, or carrying value, at which fixed assets, both tangible and intangible, are recorded in the balance sheet is the cost or valuation (fair value) less depreciation or amortisation to date.

The concept of depreciating or amortising fixed assets aims to fairly record the consumption of the asset over its useful life as economic benefit (income) is generated by the assets. The setting of the life of the assets and the method of deprecation is done as fairly as possible at the outset, but the process is subjective and business conditions do change with time, sometimes quite significantly in a very short time.

The carrying or book amount of the fixed assets may not be in line with the assets 'value to the business – that is the assets' ability to generate future cash flows. If the value to the business is higher then the fixed asset shown in the balance sheet is undervalued – that is prudent. However, if the value to the business is lower than the book amount then the fixed asset's value has been impaired – the value should be written down to the lower, more realistic and prudent amount.

A review for impairment of a fixed asset or goodwill should be carried out if events or changes in circumstance, indicate that the carrying amount of the fixed asset or goodwill, may not be recoverable.

THE CONCEPT OF RECOVERABLE AMOUNT

A prudent value for an asset would be the net disposal proceeds if it was sold, this would be the recoverable amount. However, it is obvious that simply to sell an asset would often mean getting 'scarp value' for it. The asset has a higher value if it continues in use. A means of determining this value in use is to identify the cash flows arising from the assets productive use and to discount them back to a present value. This is the value in use.

Key terms

Impairment is a reduction in the recoverable amount of a fixed asset or goodwill, below its carrying amount.

Recoverable amount is the higher of an asset's net selling price (net realizable value in UK terminology) and its value in use.

Value in use is the present value of estimated future cash flows expected to arise from the continuing use of an asset, and from its disposal at the end of its useful life.

Net realizable value is the amount at which an asset could be disposed of, less any direct selling costs.

Accounting

INDICATIONS OF IMPAIRMENT

A review for impairment of a fixed asset or goodwill, should be carried out if events or changes in circumstances indicate that the carrying amount of the fixed asset or goodwill may not be recoverable

If, and only if, the recoverable amount of an asset is less than its carrying amount, its carrying amount should be reduced to its recoverable amount. This is an impairment loss which should be recognized in the income statement. Any impairment of a previously revalued asset should be treated as a revaluation decrease.

MEASUREMENT OF IMPAIRMENT LOSSES

The Standard gives definition and clear guidance on how to calculate value in use. As far as possible the recoverable amount should be calculated for individual assets or discrete cash generating units.

There is a definition of a cash generating unit and several examples of how to determine impairment amounts, and then how to disclose impairment losses. An issue is whether the asset that is impaired was subject to previous revaluations, in which case the impairment loss can be set against that, the revalued amount, otherwise impairment losses must be charged to the income statement.

Disclosure

For each class of assets the financial statements should disclose:

a) the amount of impairment losses recognized in the income statement and under which heading the losses are included.

b) the amount of any reversals of impairment losses.

c) the amount of any impairment losses recognized in, or reversed out of, equity during the period.

If any impairment loss, or reversal of a loss, is material to the accounts **full** details of the event, circumstances should be given.

Problem areas and questions to ask about the accounts

THE SUBJECTIVITY OF FUTURE CASH FLOWS

This is a key issue and the Standard does give some guidance on what should be considered future cash flows that support the value in use of an asset. For example, future enhancement of the asset that gives rise to higher future cash flows should be excluded.

The rate at which future cash flows are discounted is also a significant parameter. Again the Standard gives some guidance.

Objective and definitions from the Standard

Objective

The objective of this Standard is to prescribe the procedures that an enterprise applies to ensure that its assets are carried at no more than their recoverable amount. An asset is carried at more than its recoverable amount if its carrying amount exceeds the amount to be recovered through use or sale of the asset. If this is the case, the asset is described as impaired and the Standard requires the enterprise recognize the impairment loss. The Standard also specifies when an enterprise should reverse an impairment loss and prescribes certain disclosures for impaired assets.

Definitions

A **recoverable amount** is the higher of an asset's net selling price and its value in use.

Value in use is the present value of estimated future cash flows expected to arise from the continuing use of an asset and from its disposal at the end of its useful life.

The **net selling price** is the amount obtainable from the sale of an asset in an arm's length transaction between knowledgeable, willing parties, less the cost of disposal.

Impairment is a reduction in the recoverable amount of a fixed asset or goodwill below its carrying amount.

An **income generating unit** is a group of assets, liabilities and associated goodwill that generates income that is largely independent of the reporting entity's other income generating streams. The assets and liabilities include those directly involved in generating the income and an appropriate portion of those used to generate more than one income stream.

Intangible assets are non-financial fixed assets that do not have physical substance but are identifiable and controlled by the entity, though custody or legal rights.

The **net realizable value** is the amount at which an asset could be disposed of, less any direct selling costs.

Purchased goodwill is the difference between the cost of an acquired entity and the aggregate of the fair values of that entity's identifiable assets and liabilities.

Readily ascertainable market value, in relation to an intangible asset, is the value that is established by reference to a market where:

a) the asset belongs to a homogeneous population of assets that are equivalent in all material respects; and

b) an active market, evidenced by frequent transactions, exists for that population.

The **recoverable amount** is the higher of net realizable value and value in use.

Tangible fixed assets are assets that have physical substance and are held for use in the production or supply of goods or services, for rental to others, or for administrative purposes on a continuing basis in the reporting entity's activities.

3.6
Construction contracts – IAS 11

Why needed

Construction projects or more generically work in progress (WIP) figures, are often a material balance sheet asset and also critical to the reporting of profits or losses at the correct amount and in the correct period. Clear definition of terms with clearly defined accounting is required.

The aim of the Standard is to ensure that work in progress is valued prudently with correct matching of revenue and costs.

Work in progress values affect both the balance sheet asset value and the related cost of sales. If you wanted to manipulate profit (and assets) then WIP valuation would be an obvious choice. For a construction contract one or all of the following may be highly subjective:

- The costs to be included.
- The stage of completion.
- Realizability of the work.

Thus the value of WIP is very often subjective. There is ample scope for manipulating figures!

Concepts

The basic concept is that costs of work done should be matched in an accounting period with the related income (or putative income), and a resultant profit or loss measured. Any costs of valuable work done and not matched by income should be carried in the balance sheet as WIP.

If you wait till the final completion and signing off of a contract or project then the profit or loss can be accurately determined. However, there is a need to calculate what profit (or loss) is being made as a project progresses. For statutory reporting purposes, it is necessary to report the profit earned in a year and the resultant asset/liability position at the balance sheet date.

A common term used in the context of contract or project sales or profits is 'earned value'. An issue with the Standard is that general principles are described but not the detailed assessment of profit (or margin) earned. The detailed definitions and calculations of 'earned value', attributable profit etc., vary considerably among companies but the principles of the measure, its calculation and uses are as follows.

The example below shows in the simplest terms the issues involved – what has to be determined and what calculations are carried out. Consistency of method is a very important issue.

Project Z		Duration 2 years		
Project sales value	a	900		
Project costs	b	820		
Expected margin	c	80		
		Year 1		**Year2**
Work done	d	480	d	340
% complete	d	480	d	340
	b	820	b	820
	=			
	e	58.54%	=	41.46%
Totals				
Margin earned	f	47	33	80
'Sales' earned	d+f	527	373	900

The above assumes that costs incurred and income earned are as originally planned or budgeted. The example ignores any costs incurred and not earned – WIP.

The Standard has examples of construction contract profit and WIP calculations in appendix A.

Key terms

Terminology – be aware that there are many alternative terms used.

Contract revenue should comprise the initial amount of revenue plus any agreed variations, claims etc.

Contract costs should comprise costs that directly relate to the specific contract, plus those that can be reasonably allocated to the contract.

Advances or progress payments are monies received from customers in respect of work done, or yet to be done. Strictly speaking these are liabilities until the contract is completed or at least has reached an agreed intermediate stage.

Retentions are monies (typically 5% or 10%) withheld by the customer in respect of advances or progress payments due. They are held until satisfactory completion of the contract. They are a debtor in a company's accounts (they may be long-term debtors).

Final estimated profit is the profit expected or anticipated to arise over the duration of the project after allowing for all costs that are not recoverable under the contract (e.g. rectification costs). This estimate may change over the life of the contract.

Attributable profit, earned value or recognized profit is that part of the final estimated profit earned to date.

Accounting

When the outcome of a construction contract can be estimated with reasonable reliability, revenue and costs should be recognized by reference to the stage of construction.

When it is probable that total costs will exceed total revenue the total expected contract loss should be recognized as an expense immediately irrespective of the stage of completion.

Disclosure

The amounts of revenue from contracts and the method of recognising this revenue should be disclosed.

For contracts in progress at the balance sheet date the following should be disclosed:

a) Costs incurred and recognized profits (or losses).

b) The amounts of advances and retentions.

Problem areas and questions to ask about the accounts

TERMINOLOGY

There are many terms used for the same figure by the companies involved with contracts. Do check out how words are being used.

STAGE OF COMPLETION

The problem here is which method to choose. The actual choice is probably not as important as ensuring consistency of application of the chosen measure.

COMPLIANCE WITH UK LAW

UK company law does not permit the inclusion of a current asset at a revalued amount, thus WIP can not carry a profit element in its value. Long-term contracts (lasting more than 12 months and thus in more than one accounting period) have to be in a sense artificially cut into annual portions. Sales and profits are earned, as in the earned value calculation, unpaid earned value is included in debtor and further costs are carried at historic cost as WIP.

COMBINING OR OFFSETTING CONTRACTS

Contracts should be treated on an individual basis. When there are material variations to a contract these should be treated as separate contracts.

COST PLUS CONTRACTS

These are not really problem areas – recognition of revenue, cost, profit or loss should be quite clear.

Any problems with fixed price contracts probably flow from the fact that the price is fixed, but the costs may not be – they are the contractor's problem! A very thorough review of the stage of completion and the costs to complete (within the fixed price) is needed.

Objective and definitions from the Standard

Objective

The objective of this Standard is to prescribe the accounting treatment of revenue and costs associated with construction contracts. Because of the nature of the activity undertaken in construction contracts, the date at which the contract activity is entered into and the date when the activity is completed, usually fall into different accounting periods. Therefore, the primary issue in accounting for construction contracts is the allocation of contract revenue and contracts costs to the accounting periods in which construction work is performed. This Standard uses the recognition criteria established in the Framework for the preparation and Presentation of Financial Statements, to determine when contract revenue and contract costs should be recognized as revenue and expenses in the income statement. It also provides practical guidance on the application of these criteria.

Definitions

A **construction contract** is a contract specifically negotiated for the construction of an asset or a combination of assets that are closely interrelated or interdependent in terms of their design, technology and output, which in some cases is subject to cost escalation clauses.

A **fixed price contract** is a construction contract in which the contractor agrees to a fixed contract price, or a fixed rate per unit of production, which in some cases is subject to cost escalation clauses.

A **cost plus contract** is a construction contract in which the contractor is reimbursed for allowable or otherwise defined costs, plus a percentage of these costs or a fixed fee.

3.7

Provisions, contingent liabilities and contingent assets – IAS 37

Why needed

To 'legally' move profits from one accounting period to another would be a very useful facility. Reported results could be in line with promised results, profits could be smoothed, losses minimized, tax charges managed and so on. The setting up and releasing of ill defined provisions could facilitate such practices. This was one of the great 'creative accounting' practices of the past.

An example of the abuse of making un-needed provisions is as follows:

- Many companies, particularly those involved in take-overs would 'over-provision' when profits were high and often equally when there were losses, make the situation really bad. They would take a 'hit' to profits or disclose a high level of losses. The promise would be increasing profits in the future once all the problems from previous deficient management had been overcome. It would not really matter whether or not the new team was as good as they claimed. There would be the high, un-needed and unused provisions to release, thus guaranteeing the promised profits (for a while at least!).

The Standard accepts the business and commercial need for provisions but brings definition as to when and how provisions should be sanctioned. The Standard demands a high degree of certainty as to cause and amount before provisions can be made.

The objective of the Standard is to ensure appropriate recognition criteria and measurement bases are applied to provisions, contingent liabilities and contingent assets, and that sufficient information is disclosed in the notes to the financial statements to enable users to understand their nature, timing and amount.

Ideas – concepts

An inherent trait of accountants is to be prudent, that is to fully anticipate all likely business costs and related liabilities whenever arising. This approach has its merits and those that are imprudent in business and accounting may not survive. Proper account should be taken of all existing and likely events and costs.

Costs and liabilities are a worry to a business – they mean that there will be an outflow of cash or depletion of other assets. Inherent caution or prudence would dictate that all reasonable, likely liabilities are recognized – a cost incurred now and a liability (provision) recognized in the balance sheet.

The prime issue which the Standard aims to address is that whilst convention and practice often dictates what is 'prudent' there is a legitimately wide range of what may be deemed 'prudent'. Costs and related liabilities should only be recognized where there is likely to be a cost and/or payment related to the event which has or will occur. Without definition and guidance too much or too little may be provided.

Key terms

A **provision** is a liability of uncertain timing or amount.

A provision is not a creditor – where you have the invoice but have not paid. It is not an accrual where there is a definite liability due now, but where the paperwork (invoice) is not available.

A provision arises when there is an obligating event – you cannot provide simply to reduce profits. The 'crystallization' or time of settlement of the liability may be some time away, also the amount of the liability may not be certain.

An **obligating event** is an event that creates a legal or constructive obligation that results in an enterprise having no realistic alternative to settling the obligation.

A **constructive obligation** occurs when practice indicates acceptance of liability, e.g. where a company makes a virtue of being environmentally responsible – they would be expected to provide for a chemical spillage, even when no law demanded such action.

A **contingent liability** is either:

- an existing obligation that is not recognized because it is unlikely that anything will have to be paid to settle the liability, or the amount of the obligation cannot be measured with sufficient reliability – it is impossible to determine an amount to provide, but such situations should be rare.

- or a possible future obligation that arises from past events and whose existence will be confirmed by the occurrence or non-occurrence, of one or more uncertain future events not wholly within the control of the enterprise.

A **contingent asset** is a possible asset that arises from past events and whose existence will be confirmed only by the occurrence or non-occurrence of one or more uncertain future events not wholly within control of the enterprise.

Accounting

A provision should be made when an enterprise has a present obligation, legal or constructive, as a result of a past event and where:

- it is probable that the provision will have to be settled; and

- a reliable estimate can be made of the amount.

If these conditions are not met then no provision should be recognized.

A provision should be the best estimate of the future liability taking account of the risks and uncertainties that surround events.

Where the effect of the time value of money is material, the amount of a provision should be the net present value of expenditure – the future costs to settle should be discounted. Guidance is given on what discount rate to use.

Gains from expected disposal of assets should not be taken into account when measuring a provision. The Standard requires that gains be treated as unrelated events. That is they should be recognized at the time of disposal of the asset.

Provisions should be reviewed at each balance sheet date to determine that they are adequate or still needed. Provisions should only be used against expenses of the event originally recognized.

An enterprise should recognize neither a contingent liability nor contingent asset.

Disclosure

PROVISIONS

For each class of provision the following should be disclosed:

a) The amount at the beginning and end of the period.

b) Details of any movements in the amounts.

c) A brief description of the nature of the obligation and expected timing of settlement.

d) The possibility of any reimbursement.

CONTINGENT LIABILITIES

For each class of contingent liability (unless a cost of settlement is extremely remote):

a) An estimate of its financial effect.

b) An indication of the uncertainties in amount and timing.

c) The possibility of any reimbursement.

CONTINGENT ASSET

Where an inflow of economic benefit is probable, an enterprise should disclose a brief description of the nature of the contingent asset. Where practicable an estimate of the amount and timing should be given.

Problem areas and questions to ask about the accounts

IS IT A LIABILITY – SHOULD YOU PROVIDE?

Traditional thinking, particularly with accountants is to be prudent. The saying 'always expect the worst and you'll never be disappointed' sums up prudence nicely. Always provide, then if bad things don't happen that is good and a provision can be released. This way of thinking can lead to un-needed, spurious provisions. This Standard requires that the liability 'outflow of economic benefits' is really more likely than not to occur.

PRESENT OBLIGATION

In rare cases it may not be clear whether there is a present obligation or not. The Standard is very helpful! It states that in such cases 'a past event is deemed to give rise to a present obligation if, taking account of all available evidence, it is more likely than not that a present obligation exists'. Examples of present obligations are court cases and guarantees.

REIMBURSED EXPENSES

Some or all of the expenditure required to settle a provision may be reimbursed by another party, e.g. an insurer. This reimbursement should only be recognized when it is virtually certain it will be received. Any certain reimbursement should be treated as a separate asset. In the income statement the provision expense may be presented net of the amount recognized as a reimbursement asset.

FUTURE OPERATING LOSSES

Provisions should not be recognized for future operating losses as a future operating loss does not meet the definition of a liability. A business does not have an obligation to make a loss!

ONEROUS CONTRACTS

If an entity has a contract that is onerous, the present obligation under the contract should be recognized and measured as a provision. An onerous contract is a contract in which the unavoidable costs of meeting the obligations under it exceed the economic benefits expected to be received under it. The unavoidable costs under a contract reflect the least cost of exiting from the contract, i.e. the lower of the cost of fulfilling it and any compensation, or penalties arising from failure to fulfill it.

Many normal contracts, e.g. to construct a building, might be onerous in that the contract might be fixed price with a clearly defined specification. If the contractor has misjudged the soil conditions and thus the cost of foundations, then he will still have to deliver the contract to specification and for the fixed price – the contract has become onerous to the contractor.

RESTRUCTURING COSTS

Provision can only be made for restructuring costs where there is a constructive obligation to carry out the restructuring. That is, where there is a detailed plan that will be implemented and there is a valid expectation in those affected that the restructuring will proceed. In other words, where the restructuring has been publicly announced.

PREJUDICING YOUR CASE

In extremely rare cases, disclosing some or all of the information required by the Standard might seriously prejudice the negotiations and outcome of a dispute. In such cases the enterprise need not disclose the information, but should disclose the general nature of the dispute, together with the fact that, and reason why, the information has not been disclosed.

DIFFERENCES IN GAAP

Provision or reserve? There can be possible differences in GAAP where some countries allow amounts to be 'reserved', e.g. banks could hold secret reserves – or provisions. When looking at accounts (presumably not fully complying with IFRS's) a review of reserves is sensible.

Objective and definitions from the Standard

Objective

The objective of this Standard is to ensure that appropriate recognition criteria and measurement bases are applied to provisions, contingent liabilities and contingent assets and that sufficient information is disclosed in the notes to the financial statements to enable users to understand their nature, timing and amount.

Definitions

A **provision** is a liability of uncertain timing or amount.

A **liability** is a present obligation of the enterprise arising from past events, the settlement of which is expected to result in an outflow from the enterprise of resources embodying economic benefits.

An **obligating event** is an event that creates a legal or constructive obligation that results in an enterprise having no realistic alternative to settling the obligation

A legal obligation is an obligation that derives from:

a) a contract (through its explicit or implicit terms);

b) legislation; or

c) other operation of law.

A **constructive obligation** is an obligation that derives from an enterprise's actions where:

a) by an established pattern of past practice, published policies or a sufficiently specific current statement, the enterprise has indicated to other parties that it will accept certain responsibilities; and

b) as a result the enterprise has created a valid expectation on the part of those other parties that it will discharge those responsibilities.

A **contingent liability** is:

a) a possible obligation that arises from past events and whose existence will be confirmed by the occurrence or non-occurrence of one or more uncertain future events not wholly within the control of the enterprise; or

b) a present obligation that arises from past events but is not recognized because:

   i) it is not probable that an outflow of resources embodying economic benefits will be required to settle the obligation; or

   ii) the amount of the obligation cannot be measured with sufficient reliability.

A **contingent asset** is a possible asset that arises from past events and whose existence will be confirmed only by the occurrence or non-occurrence, of one or more uncertain future events not wholly within control of the enterprise.

An **onerous contract** is a contract in which the unavoidable costs of meeting the obligations under the contract exceed the economic benefits expected to be received under it.

A **restructuring** is a programme that is planned and controlled by management, and materially changes either:

a) the scope of a business undertaken by an enterprise; or

b) the manner in which that business is conducted.

3.8
The effects of changes in foreign exchange rates – IAS 21

Why needed

Trade is carried on between countries that have different currencies that continually fluctuate in relative value. There are many possible ways of translating financial statements in one currency into those of another. The issue is how to report a period's results and balance sheet position when exchange rates fluctuate.

Ideas – concepts

The underlying principal should be that results and assets and liabilities should not be distorted in amount simply through using an inappropriate translation method or exchange rate. The aim must be to present the figures in the accounts of the reporting entity's currency as fairly as possible. Thus transactions should be translated at the rate ruling at the date of the transaction. Balance sheet figures should be translated at the rate ruling at the balance sheet date. For non-monetary (fixed) assets and liabilities the historical rate should be used.

FOREIGN ENTITIES – NET INVESTMENT APPROACH

A common way to mitigate the effect of changes in exchange rates is to purchase the foreign assets (investment in an entity) by means of a loan taken out in the same foreign currency. Thus any change in the asset value on translation should be more or less off-set by a compensating change in liability amount – this is an example of hedging.

Key terms

Translation is the act of changing amounts in one currency into those of another on paper, whereas conversion is the act of physically changing amounts of currency.

Functional currency is the currency of the primary economic environment in which the entity operates.

Foreign currency is a currency other than the functional currency of an entity.

Presentation currency is the currency in which the financial statements are presented.

Exchange rate is the ratio of exchange of two currencies.

Spot exchange rate is the rate for immediate delivery.

Closing rate is the spot exchange rate at the balance sheet date.

Exchange difference is the difference resulting from reporting the same number of units of a foreign currency in the reporting currency at different exchange rates.

Foreign operation is an entity that is a subsidiary, associate joint venture or branch of the reporting entity, the activities of which are based or conducted in a country other than the country of the reporting entity.

Net investment in a foreign operation is the amount of the reporting entity's interest in the net assets of that operation.

Accounting

INITIAL RECOGNITION
Foreign currency transactions shall be recorded on initial recognition in the functional currency, by applying to the foreign currency amount the spot exchange rate at the date of the transaction.

AT SUBSEQUENT BALANCE SHEET DATES
Monetary items shall be translated using the closing rate.

Non-monetary items that are measured at historical cost in a foreign currency shall be translated using the exchange rate at the date of the transaction.

Non-monetary items that are measured at fair value in foreign currency shall be translated using the exchange rate at the date when the fair value was determined.

Disclosure

An enterprise should disclose:

a) the amount of exchange difference included in the net profit or loss for the period

b) net exchange differences that are classified as changes in equity with a reconciliation of the amount of the differences at the beginning and end of the period

If the presentation currency is different from the functional currency an explanation should be given.

Problem areas and questions to ask about the accounts

VOLUME OF TRANSACTION

For businesses trading daily in different currencies there can be problems where exchange rates change by the minute. With the cheapness and ease of computerized accounting this may not be a problem. It may be acceptable to use an average rate for a day, or for short periods, to facilitate accounting.

SEVERE DEVALUATION OF A CURRENCY

The Standard allows such exchange differences to be included in the carrying amount of relevant assets.

Objective and definitions from the Standard

Objective

An entity may carry on foreign activities in two ways. It may have transactions in foreign currencies or it may have foreign operations. In addition, an entity may present its financial statements in a foreign currency. The objective of this Standard is to prescribe how to include foreign currency transactions and foreign operations in the financial statements of an entity and how to translate financial statements into a presentation currency.

The principal issues are to decide which exchange rate(s) to use and how to report the effect of changes in exchange rates in the financial statements.

Definitions

Functional currency is the currency of the primary economic environment in which the entity operates.

Foreign currency is a currency other than the functional currency of an entity.

Presentational currency is the currency in which the financial statements are presented.

Exchange rate is the ratio of exchange of two currencies.

Spot exchange rate is the rate for immediate delivery.

Closing rate is the spot exchange rate at the balance sheet date.

Exchange difference is the difference resulting from reporting the same number of units of a foreign currency in the reporting currency at different exchange rates.

Foreign operation is an entity that is a subsidiary, associate joint venture or branch of the reporting entity, the activities of which are based or conducted in a country other than the country of the reporting entity.

Net investment in a foreign operation is the amount of the reporting entity's interest in the net assets of that operation.

Monetary items are money held and assets and liabilities to be received or paid in fixed or determinable amounts of money.

Fair value is the amount for which an asset could be exchanged between knowledgeable, willing parties in an arm's length transaction.

3.9

Income taxes – IAS12

Why needed

Where tax is levied it obviously has to be charged as a cost matched with the profits or gains to which it relates. However, tax laws do not always result in tax being charged on the accounting profit shown, or at rates and times that match the accounting profit. Thus to understand the tax charge in financial statements there is inevitably need for disclosures of the basis of the charge.

A particular timing issue may arise in many countries due to favourable tax depreciation charges – 'writing down allowances' for fixed assets. These generous allowances are given against profits, the aim being to encourage investment in fixed assets and infrastructure. When a company purchases new assets and benefits from the generous writing down allowances, the tax that has to be paid may be much lower than that indicated by the prevailing rate for taxes on profits. This is because the tax authorities ignore, that is, add back the accounting depreciation charges and substitute their own, more generous allowance. Over the period of asset ownership the same amount of tax has to be paid – less in earlier years as the actual tax is deferred, but more in later years – this is deferred tax.

There may be other distortions and anomalies arising out of a particular tax regime – these should be disclosed.

Ideas – concepts

TAXABLE PROFITS

The accounting profit or loss disclosed in a set of financial statements is rarely the profit or loss on which tax is charged. Whether an expense is allowable or income is taxable and when any tax is payable, often differs from the basis used in accounts preparation. Examples:

* interest earned or paid is often taxed on a cash rather than accruals basis;
* expenses for entertainment or parking fines, whilst costs of business are considered disallowable expenses by tax authorities.

DEFERRED TAX

A simple example is set out at the end of this chapter. Even with very simple figures as in the example it takes time to work through. The point is that over the full life of an asset purchased and fully depreciated, the total tax charge should be the same. With generous tax writing down allowances the tax to be paid is lower in the earlier years, but this is balanced by increasing charges at the end of the assets life. The payment of the tax is deferred but the total tax liability over the asset's life is the same. A good way of describing this is to call the deferred tax provision account a 'tax equalisation' account.

The aim of the Standard is to disclose how tax charges and liabilities are compiled – to reconcile the differences between normal accruals accounting and tax accounting.

Note: there is a movement by the Inland Revenue to align tax accounting with accounting which follows IAS.

Key terms

CURRENT TAX

The amount of tax estimated to be payable or recoverable in respect of the taxable profit or loss for a period, along with adjustments to estimates of previous periods.

TIMING DIFFERENCES

Differences between an entity's taxable profits and its results, as stated in the financial statements that arise from the inclusion of gains and losses in tax assessments, in periods different from those in which they are recognized in financial statements.

DEFERRED TAX LIABILITIES

Estimated future tax consequences of transactions and events recognized in the financial statements of the current and previous periods.

PERMANENT DIFFERENCES

Differences between an entity's taxable profits and its results, as stated in the financial statements that arise because certain types of income and expenditure are non-taxable or disallowable, or because certain tax charges or allowances have no corresponding amount in the financial statements.

Accounting

Current tax due, whether for current or past periods, should be charged in the income statement and recognized as a liability. Any benefit relating to a tax loss that can be carried back to recover tax paid of a previous period, should be credited to the income statement and recognized as an asset.

A **deferred tax liability** should be recognized for all taxable temporary differences and charged to the income statement.

A **deferred tax asset** should be recognized to the extent that it is probable that taxable profit will be available in the future against which to recover tax, or reduce liability.

Disclosure

An explanation of the relationship between tax expense (income) and accounting profit.

An explanation of changes in the applicable tax rate(s) compared with the previous accounting period.

The amount of any deductible temporary differences, unused tax losses and unused tax credits, for which no deferred tax asset is recognized in the balance sheet.

Problem areas and questions to ask about your accounts

WHAT IS A DEFERRED TAX LIABILITY, WHEN WILL IT BE PAID?

The international and equivalent and recently revised (2000) UK Standards, all require full provision to be made for the future tax liability. BUT if a company continues to grow, at a reasonable and sustainable rate, then the deferred tax is not going to payable, the provision – liability will not crystallize and simply grow in amount. The former UK approach was to take a view on what the liability might really be and provide only that amount. The Standard setters have in my view taken the easy option and demanded full provision be made. It will be interesting to see how many companies have ever growing deferred tax liabilities – will these be true liabilities? How will analysts view these long-term liabilities which are unlikely ever to be settled by payment of cash to the tax authorities?

DISCOUNTING THE FUTURE LIABILITY

The recent UK and other countries' Standards acknowledged that the liability to pay tax was in the future and thus, a truer view of the present liability would be to discount year by year the possible future liabilities. The IAS does not allow discounting – this does cut out some subjectivity, for example what discount rate to use. BUT this again leaves the situation that deferred tax liabilities may not be as real as other liabilities shown in the balance sheet.

TAXATION DISCLOSURES FOR INVESTMENT COMPANIES AND GROUPS

The tax charge (credits) and liabilities (assets) for a group may be complex. The Standard requires additional disclosure in such cases.

DIFFERENCES IN GAAP

Differences in tax figures are much more likely to be affected by differences in tax laws. The IAS eliminates differences in accounting for deferred tax.

Objective and definitions used in the Standard

Objective

The objective of this Standard is to prescribe the accounting treatment for income taxes. The principal issue in accounting for income taxes is how to account for current and future tax consequences of:

a) the future recovery (settlement) of the carrying amount of assets (liabilities) that are recognized in an enterprise's balance sheet; and

b) transactions and other events of the current period that are recognized in an enterprise's financial statements.

Definitions

Accounting profit is net profit or loss for a period before deducting tax expense

Taxable profit (tax loss) is the profit (loss) for a period, determined in accordance with the rules established by the taxation authorities, upon which income taxes are payable (recoverable).

Tax expense (tax income) is the aggregate amount included in the determination of net profit or loss for the period in respect of current and deferred tax.

Current tax is the amount of income taxes payable (recoverable) in respect of the taxable profit (tax loss) for a period.

Deferred tax liabilities are the amounts of income taxes payable in future periods in respect of temporary taxable differences.

Deferred tax assets are the amounts of income taxes recoverable in future periods in respect of:

a) deductible temporary differences;

b) the carry forward of unused tax losses; and

c) the carry forward of unused tax credits.

Temporary differences are differences between the carrying amount of an asset or liability in the balance sheet and its tax base. Temporary differences may be either:

a) **taxable temporary differences** which are temporary differences that will result in taxable amounts in determining taxable profit (tax loss) of future periods, when the carrying amount of the asset or liability is recovered or settled; or

b) **deductible temporary differences** which are temporary differences that will result in amounts that are deductible in determining taxable profit (tax loss) of future periods when the carrying amount of the asset or liability is recovered or settled.

The **tax base** of an asset or liability is the amount attributed to that asset or liability for tax purposes.

3.10
Employee benefits – IAS19

Why needed

The cost of providing pensions is often very significant, especially where the pension is a guaranteed amount linked to the final salary level of the employee. To provide for these future liabilities amounts are set aside in a separate managed fund, sufficient to cover the likely cost of all pension commitments. When a company is growing and successful, with an expanding workforce in a generally growing economy, then presumably the funds put aside will grow (the investments will give returns that are reinvested) sufficiently to cover all future pension liabilities. BUT what happens in a stagnant business, in a stagnant economy where investment returns are poor? The answer: inadequate funds to meet future pension liabilities.

There are also other types of employee benefit (including salaries, redundancy or termination benefits etc.) for which the accounting may need to be clearly defined. But it is the funding of pensions that is the most controversial – causing the biggest cost to companies, possibly there will be huge liabilities. This is real concern to businesses, governments, employees and pensioners.

Ideas – concepts

Defined benefit pension schemes potentially offer employees financial security in retirement, but at a present cost to the company. The actual liability may be deferred, but the cost of meeting should be charged to the income statement now. It is the present liability of the company that needs to be known and revealed. This liability manifests itself year by year in the amounts needed to be charged to the income statement to build up a sufficient fund to meet the future pension liabilities.

Liabilities, particularly future liabilities, should be fully accounted for and disclosed. Promises to provide pensions are very real commitments and the liability attaching should be calculated and accounted for.

IF the following were know with certainty:

- the life expectancy of retirees;
- the amounts payable each year (possibly adjusted for inflation); and
- the returns on funds invested;

then actuaries could with confidence say how much should be invested each year to provide the funds necessary to meet the calculated future liabilities.

All of the above data are to a degree subjective, but it is the returns on funds invested, that in the last few years has not just been uncertain, but sharply declining from that which had been confidently anticipated.

Key terms

Defined contribution schemes or plans (also known as money purchase schemes) are pension plans under which an enterprise pays fixed contributions into a separate entity (a fund), and has no legal or constructive obligation to pay further contributions. Amounts to be paid as pensions are determined by contributions to a fund, together with investment earnings thereon.

Defined benefit plans are pension plans other than defined contribution plans. They are pension schemes or plans under which amounts to be paid as pensions are determined by reference to a formula, usually based on employee's earnings and/or years of service.

Actuarial gains and losses arise from changes in actuarial assumptions. Actual or experience changes are the effect of differences between the previous actuarial assumptions and what has actually occurred – e.g. stock market returns were assumed to be 10% but only 7% is now being achieved.

The **present value** of fund assets or pension obligations is the present amount of the assets or liabilities. Present value is found by discounting the future amounts using an appropriate discount rate.

The **discount rate**. Defined benefit scheme liabilities should be discounted at a rate that reflects the time value of money and the characteristics of the liability. Such a rate should be assumed to be the current rate of return on a high quality corporate bond (AAA) of equivalent currency and term to the scheme liabilities.

Accounting

SHORT-TERM EMPLOYEE BENEFITS

Accounting for short-term employee benefits is generally straightforward.

Amounts due in respect of employee costs for salaries, wages, holiday pay, medical benefits, etc. should be accounted for as a cost. That is an expense in the income statement, and as a liability in the balance sheet if unpaid at the period end.

Post-employment benefits – pensions

DEFINED CONTRIBUTION PLANS

Amounts due as contributions to defined contribution schemes should be accounted for as a cost. That is an expense in the income statement, and as a liability in the balance sheet if unpaid at the period end.

If contributions are not due to be paid over into the fund until after the end of the period, the amounts due should be discounted using the prescribed discount rate.

DEFINED BENEFIT PLANS

The amount recognized as a defined benefit liability should be the net sum of the present value of the defined benefit obligations, less the fair value of the pension fund (plan assets) as at the balance sheet date.

This simple requirement may be complicated by the inclusion of a liability for change in pension conditions – past service costs, e.g. when the benefits of a pension are increased from 2% to 2.5% per year of service.

The existing IAS 19 allows the effect of actuarial gains, or more importantly actuarial losses, to be moderated so that a sudden fall in the fair value of the pension fund assets does not have to be charged as a one off, but rather spread. This aspect of the Standard is likely to be removed, so that any changes in fair value of funds will hit the income statement when they occur. This has become a very emotive issue in the past few years due particularly to the severe fall in equity market values. The Standard setters do seem intent upon changes in liability being recognized immediately they occur. This does seem odd, as it is extremely prudent and the life cycle of a pension scheme would allow for adjustments to be made over time. BUT the trouble is that many businesses might never make the necessary adjustments and adequately fund their pension commitments.

Disclosure

DEFINED CONTRIBUTION PLANS

The amounts paid into a defined contribution pension scheme should be disclosed.

DEFINED BENEFIT PLANS

The following should be disclosed in respect of defined benefit schemes:

a) The accounting policy for recognizing actuarial gains and losses.

b) A general description of the pension plan.

c) An analysis of the balance sheet pension related assets and liabilities.

d) Any pension plan assets that are those of the enterprise, either financial instruments of property or other assets used by the enterprise.

e) A reconciliation of movements during the year in net liability.

f) An analysis of the total pension plan related expenses in the income statement.

g) The actual return on pension plan assets.

h) The principal actuarial assumptions used as at the balance sheet date.

Problem areas and questions to ask about the accounts

SUBJECTIVITY OF DATA

The fact that actuarial computations require many assumptions means that figures for pension liabilities can cover quite a range. The Standard does gives guidance on the need for tight definition of assumptions.

CONSTRUCTIVE OBLIGATIONS

A business should account not only for its legal obligations under a defined benefit plan but also for any constructive obligations. Such constructive obligations may arise from the informal, but established practices of a business – e.g. if the business has for years always increased pension payments in line with the retail price index, even though no such condition exists in the formal pension agreement.

EQUITY COMPENSATION BENEFITS

Share or stock options have hit the headlines over the past few years. Are these really salary or, as many would say, merely incentives!

Many schemes where the options (given for no consideration or modest payment) are modest in amount and widely distributed could be considered as loyalty schemes, rewarding executives and staff for long-term commitment.

However, many schemes undoubtedly are a means of remunerating executives and staff. They have the following advantages for a business: there is no cash outlay on salaries, it is merely paper! There may also be payroll and other taxation (minimization) benefits to both the business and the recipient.

Current thought is that equity compensation should be somehow shown as an income statement charge as it is effectively remuneration. There are IFRS and national exposure drafts on this topic.

At present IAS 19 gives guidance about disclosure of any equity compensation schemes.

CONTRIBUTIONS TO MULTI-EMPLOYER OR STATE SCHEMES

Where contributions are made to a scheme (a fund) which exists for the benefit of more than one business's employees, the Standard gives guidance on how contributions, liabilities etc. are to be accounted for and disclosed. In essence these schemes will really be as a single enterprise's scheme – to be accounted for either as a defined contribution or defined benefit scheme.

IS THE BUSINESS UNDER REVIEW DISCLOSING ALL PENSION LIABILITIES?

The EU fourth Directive seems to allow that pension liabilities be merely noted in financial statements. There may be businesses which are not accounting for their true liabilities. Presumably this will change when they adopt IAS 19?

Objective and definitions from the Standard

Objective

The objective of this Standard is to prescribe the accounting and disclosure for employee benefits. The Standard requires an enterprise to recognize:

a) liability when an employee has provided service in exchange for employee benefits to be paid in the future; and

b) an expense when the enterprise consumes the economic benefit arising from service provided by an employee, in exchange for employee benefits.

Definitions

Employee benefits are all forms of consideration given by an enterprise in exchange for service rendered by employees.

Short-term employee benefits are employee benefits (other than termination benefits and equity compensation benefits) which fall due wholly within twelve months after the end of the period in which the employees render the related service.

Post employment benefits are employee benefits (other than termination benefits and equity compensation benefits) which are payable after the completion of employment.

Post employment benefit plans are formal or informal arrangements under which an enterprise provides post employment benefits for one or more employees.

Defined contribution plans are post employment benefit plans under which an enterprise pays fixed contributions into a separate entity (a fund), and will have no legal or constructive obligation to pay further contributions if the fund does not hold sufficient assets to pay all employee benefits relating to employee service in the current and prior periods.

Defined benefit plans are post employment benefit plans other than defined contribution plans.

Multi-employer plans are defined contribution plans (other than state plans) or defined benefit plans (other than state plans) that:

a) pool the assets contributed by various enterprises that are not under common control; and

b) use those assets to provide benefits to employees of more than one enterprise, on the basis that contribution and benefit levels are determined without regard to the identity of the enterprise that employs the employees concerned.

Other long-term employee benefits are employee benefits (other than post employment benefits, termination benefits and equity compensation benefits) which do not fall due wholly within twelve months after the end of the period in which the employees render the related service.

Termination benefits are employee benefits payable as a result of either:

a) an enterprise's decision to terminate an employee's employment before normal retirement date; or

b) an employee's decision to accept voluntary redundancy in exchange for those benefits.

Equity compensation benefits are employee benefits under which either:

a) employees are entitled to receive equity financial instruments issued by the enterprise (or its parent); or

b) the amount of the enterprise's obligation to employees depends on the future price of equity financial instruments issued by the enterprise.

Equity compensation plans are formal or informal arrangements under which an enterprise provides equity compensation benefits for one or more employees.

Vested employee benefits are employee benefits that are not conditional on future employment.

The **present value** of a defined benefit obligation is the present value, without deducting any plan assets, of expected future payments required to settle the obligation resulting from employee service in the current and prior periods.

The **current service cost** is the increase in the present value of the defined obligation resulting from employee service in the current period.

The **interest cost** is the increase during a period in the present value of a defined benefit obligation, which arises because the benefits are one period closer to settlement.

Assets held by a long-term employee benefit fund are assets (other than non-transferable financial instruments issued by the reporting enterprise) that:

a) are held by an entity (a fund) that is legally separate from the reporting enterprise and exists solely to pay off fund employee benefits; and

b) are available to be used only to pay or fund employee benefits, are not available to the reporting enterprise's own creditors (even in bankruptcy), and cannot be returned to the reporting enterprise, unless either:

    i)   the remaining assets of the fund are sufficient to meet all the related employee benefit obligations of the plan or the reporting enterprise; or

    ii) the assets are returned to the reporting enterprise to reimburse it for employee benefits already paid.

A **qualifying insurance policy** is an insurance policy issued by an insurer that is not a related party (as defined in IAS 24 Related Party Disclosures) of the reporting enterprise, if the proceeds of the policy:

a) can be used only to pay or fund employee benefits under a defined benefit plan; and

b) are not available to the reporting enterprises own creditors (even in bankruptcy) and cannot be paid to the reporting enterprise, unless either:

    i)   the proceeds represent surplus assets that are not needed for the policy to meet all the related employee benefit obligations; or

    ii) the proceeds are returned to the reporting enterprise to reimburse it for employee benefits already paid.

Fair value is the amount for which an asset could be exchanged or a liability settled between knowledgeable, willing parties in an arm's length transaction.

The **return on plan assets** is interest, dividends and other revenue derived from the plan assets, together with realized and unrealized gains or losses on the plan assets, less any costs of administering the plan and less any tax payable by the plan itself.

Actuarial gains and losses comprise:

a) experience adjustments (the effects of differences between the previous actuarial assumptions and what has actually occurred); and

b) the effect of changes in actuarial assumptions.

Past service cost is the increase in the present value of the defined benefit obligation for the employee service in prior periods, resulting in the current period from the introduction of, or changes to, post employment benefits or other long-term employee benefits. Past service cost may be either positive (where benefits are introduced or improved) or negative (where existing benefits are reduced).

FOUR

Creative accounting

4.1

Revenue – IAS18

Why needed

Revenue (income, sales or turnover) is the life blood of business. All businesses want more! For cash sales in a shop the revenue earned is clear, or is it? Even there, there might be a history of returned goods which, 'as the customer is always right' will give rise to refunds. So when is revenue accurately determined and irrevocably earned? That is the question.

The primary issues in accounting for revenue are the correct classification of credits as income and the timing of recognition. The definition in the Accounting Standard does not really help, it merely states the obvious. 'Revenue is recognized when it is probable that future economic benefits will flow to the enterprise and these benefits can be measured reliably'. This Standard does go on to identify the circumstances under which these criteria will be met and, therefore, revenue will be recognized. It also provides practical guidance on the application of these criteria.

Income recognition should be neither inappropriately deferred nor, what is more prevalent, anticipated.

Ideas – concepts

Revenue (income or sales) and the net of costs figure of earnings or profits are vital figures when reporting a businesses progress. There will always be pressure to show the highest, most favourable position.

More fundamentally the bedrock concept of accruals demands that revenue and costs be properly matched within the time period being reported upon. There must be clear rules on what is the genuine revenue earned in any accounting period.

Key terms

Revenue is the gross inflow of economic benefits during the period arising in the course of the ordinary activities of an enterprise when those inflows result in increases in equity, other than increases relating to contributions from equity participants.

Accounting

Accounting for revenue should be obvious and can be understood by considering the key demands of the Standard:

- **Revenue should not be overstated in amount**
  Revenue should be measured at the fair value of the consideration received or receivable and the amount of revenue can be measured reliably.

- **Revenue will flow to the seller, has indeed been earned**
  An enterprise has transferred to the buyer the significant risks and rewards of ownership of the goods and it is probable that the economic benefits associated with the transaction will flow to the enterprise.

The Standard reiterates these bases for accounting for different classes of revenue and the text from the Standard is set out below.

For the sale of goods revenue should be recognized when:

a) the enterprise has transferred to the buyer the significant risks and rewards of ownership of the goods;

b) the enterprise retains neither continuing managerial involvement to the degree usually associated with ownership, nor effective control over the goods sold;

c) the amount of revenue can be measured reliably;

d) it is probable that the economic benefits associated with the transaction will flow to the enterprise; and

e) the costs incurred, or to be incurred, in respect of the transaction can be measured reliably.

For rendering of services when the outcome of a transaction can be estimated reliably, revenue associated with the transaction should be recognized by reference to the stage of completion of the transaction at the balance sheet date. The outcome of a transaction can be estimated reliably when all the following conditions are satisfied:

a) the amount of revenue can be measured reliably;

b) it is probable that the economic benefits associated with the transaction will flow to the enterprise;

c) the stage of completion of the transaction at the balance sheet date can be measured reliably; and

d) the costs incurred for the transaction and the costs to complete the transaction, can be measured reliably.

When the outcome of the transaction involving the rendering of services cannot be estimated reliably, revenue should be recognized only to the extent of expenses recognized that are recoverable.

Interest, royalties and dividends should be recognized on the following basis:

a) it is probable that the economic benefits associated with the transaction will flow to the enterprise;

b) the amount of revenue can be measured reliably;

c) interest should be recognized on a time proportion basis that takes into account the effective yield on the asset;

d) royalties should be recognized on an accrual basis in accordance with the substance of the relevant agreement; and

e) dividends should be recognized when the shareholder's right to receive payment is established.

This Standard is in the process of being revised. A recent UK exposure draft on an Application Note on Revenue and IAS Interpretations deals with specific revenue recognition issues.

Disclosure

An enterprise should disclose:

- **the accounting policies adopted** for recognition of revenue; and

- **revenue by significant category**, e.g. sale of goods, rendering of services etc.

If relevant details of revenue arising from exchange of goods or services under each appropriate category.

Problem areas and questions to ask about the accounts

TIMING OF SALE

This may often be a problem. Take for example deposits received for goods or services – when do these become earned revenue? Contract or taxation laws maybe pointers, but not conclusively so. An example UK VAT law requires that sales normally be invoiced with in 14 days of the supply of good or services, however, a company may accept that the goods are really sold when approved of or accepted by the customer.

For the majority of business situations the timing of sale will be clear and the Standard and Interpretations are being developed to deal with difficult or more contentious situations.

DIFFERENCES IN GAAP

This is a Standard that is being reviewed. The topic was not covered by a specific UK Standard.

Objective and definitions from the Standard

Objective

Income is defined in the Framework for the Preparation and Presentation of Financial Statements as increases in economic benefits during the accounting period in the form of inflows, or enhancements of assets, or decreases of liabilities that result in increases in equity, other than those relating to contributions from equity participants. Income encompasses both revenue and gains. Revenue is income that arises in the course of ordinary activities of an enterprise and is referred to by a variety of different names, including sales, fees, interest, dividends and royalties. The objective of this Standard is to prescribe the accounting treatment of revenue arising from certain types of transactions and events.

The primary issue in accounting for revenue is determining when to recognize revenue. Revenue is recognized when it is probable that future economic benefits will flow to the enterprise and these benefits can be measured reliably. This Standard identifies the circumstances in which these criteria will be met and, therefore, revenue will be recognized. It also provides practical guidance on the application of these criteria.

Definitions

Revenue is the gross inflow of economic benefits during the period arising in the course of the ordinary activities of an enterprise when those inflows result in increases in equity, other than increases relating to contributions from equity participants.

Fair Value is the amount for which an asset could be exchanged, or a liability settled, between knowledgeable, willing parties in an arm's length transaction.

4.2

Leases – IAS 17

Why needed

Many businesses obtain use of assets through leases and hire purchase agreements. If a company showed leased asset costs as an expense then profits would be lower, but there would be neither assets nor the contra liabilities on the balance sheet. Capital employed would be lower and the corollary would be that there would be no financing shown – less money borrowed by the company. This is an example of 'off-balance sheet finance'.

Liabilities could be hidden, gearing would appear lower and performance measures distorted.

Ideas – concepts

The Standard is based on the concept of 'substance over form' and thus requires that leased assets be brought onto the balance sheet along with the contra liability. (*See chapter 9.4 for a more detailed explanation and example.*)

Assets leased, hired or rented for a fixed, non-cancellable period equivalent to their useful lives are in substance purchased assets. The bank or finance house financing the asset certainly does not consider it owns an asset, but rather that it has a debtor – a loan repayable over time. The bank is merely a financial intermediary. Would the bank manager be happy if a business returned its fleet of leased dumper trucks and left them on the doorstep?

The business has purchased and will use the assets for all of, or the best part of, their useful lives. These assets are capital employed of the business. But possibly more significant is the fact that the business has irrevocably committed to make, for example, say 36 monthly payments – they have in effect a 3 year loan. This commitment – liability should be shown. This is borrowed capital invested in the business.

Key terms

LEASE

A lease is a contract between a lessor and a lessee for the hire of a specific asset. The lessor retains ownership of the asset but conveys the right of use of the asset to the lessee for an agreed period of time in return for the payment of specified rentals. This is usually because the lease term covers most of the useful life of the asset.

FINANCE LEASE

A finance lease is a lease that transfers substantially all the risks and rewards of ownership of an asset to the lessee.

OPERATING LEASE

An operating lease is a lease other than a finance lease. It could be likened to a short-term rental agreement; one for say 12 months but that can be cancelled at short notice.

Accounting – in the accounts of the lessee

A finance lease should be recorded in the balance sheet of a lessee as an asset and as an equal liability – an obligation to pay future rentals. At the inception of the lease the sum to be recorded both as an asset and as a liability, should be the fair value of the leased asset or, if lower, the present value of the minimum lease payments.

Leased assets should be depreciated. The depreciation policy should be consistent with that for depreciable assets which are owned (as set out in IAS 16 Property, Plant and Equipment).

Lease charges should be apportioned between finance charge and the reduction of the outstanding liability. The finance charge should be allocated to periods during the lease term so as to produce a constant periodic rate of interest over the term of the liability. This means using compound interest calculations with high interest and low capital payments at the inception of the lease and the reverse towards the end of the term of the liability.

Operating lease rents should be charged on a straight line basis over the lease term, unless some other systematic basis is more appropriate.

Disclosure – In the accounts of the Lessee

A general description of the lessee's significant leasing arrangements.

The gross amount of leased assets and related depreciation of leased assets should be disclosed. Obligations to make minimum lease payments should be analyzed in bands of current, 2-5 years and over 5 years. The present value (of the capital element) of the payments should also be made in the same bandings. A reconciliation between the two sets of bandings should also be given – this will represent the future interest payable on the loans.

The finance charges for leased assets should be separately disclosed.

Details of any sub leases, restrictions or contingent liabilities associated with leasing.

Accounting – In the accounts of the Lessor

FINANCE LEASES

As the lessor is the other party to the lease the accounting is essentially the mirror image of lessee accounting.

For a finance lease, the amount due from a lessee should be recorded in the balance sheet as a receivable or debtor at the amount of the net investment in the lease.

The recognition of finance income should be based on a pattern reflecting a constant periodic rate of return on the lessor's net investment outstanding in respect of the finance lease. This means using compound interest calculations with high interest and low capital receipts at the inception of the lease and the reverse towards the end of the term of the liability.

If the lessor is a manufacturer or dealer in leased assets the profit on the sale of the asset should be recognized as for an outright sale. If artificially low rates of lease interest are quoted then the profit on the sale should be restricted to that which would apply if a commercial interest rate were charged.

OPERATING LEASES

Lessors should present assets which are leased out under operating leases in their balance sheets under the appropriate heading.

Operating lease income should be recognized in incom
straight line basis over the lease term, unless some other s
more appropriate.

Disclosure – In the accounts of the Lessor

The total gross investment in the lease and the present valu~ or minimum lease payments receivable at the balance sheet date should be analyzed in bands of current, 2-5 years and over 5 years.

The policy for accounting for leases, the aggregate rentals receivable, the unearned finance income due and any accumulated allowance (provision) for payments due that are considered uncollectible minimum lease payments, should all be disclosed.

Problem areas and questions to ask about the accounts

IS IT A FINANCE LEASE OR NOT?

Finance leases prevent off-balance sheet finance and the consequent hiding of borrowing. Thus one of their major attractions is lost. There are still many other attractions such as: more evenly spread and manageable cash flows (no up- front payment for assets); reducing the risks of ownership of assets; possible tax advantages.

But taking borrowing (and the contra capital employed) off the balance sheet is a major driver for leasing companies financing leased assets, and their customers who lease the assets. Over the years clever schemes and lease contracts have been devised to get round this Standard.

The Standard is being reviewed and will be tightened up even further, even possibly to the extent of including long-term leased buildings as 'owned' assets.

This revision is not expected until 2006 at the earliest.

g assets to a third party and leasing them back is an acceptable and ften sensible means of raising finance. The issue is how to deal with any profit or loss (proceeds from the sale less the carrying value of the assets) at the time of sale. If the terms of the lease back are such that the lease is a finance lease then any profit arising should be spread over the life of the lease. The asset remains on the balance sheet and an amount equivalent to the cash received is set up as a loan creditor.

Profits or losses on the sale to a third party where an operating lease is deemed to exist should be recognized in the income statement immediately.

The Standard has a guidance appendix on this issue.

HIRE PURCHASE CONTRACTS

These are dealt with as for finance leases.

PFI (PRIVATE FINANCE INITIATIVE) PPP (PUBLIC PRIVATE PARTNERSHIPS) AND THE LIKE

No matter what one's view on the politics of Private Finance Initiatives (PFI), PPP and similar contracts, they have achieved UK and international acceptance as a means of helping to satisfy demand for public assets and services. The greatest problem with PFI projects is the determination of whether or not they do pass risk from the Treasury (tax payer) to third parties. It would be simple enough to define events and related cash flows in such a way that the contract was definitely 'off balance sheet', that is neither an asset of nor a corresponding liability of the Treasury (the taxpayer). However, a major thrust of accounting and financial reporting in the last few years has been to prevent entities (commercial companies) from hiding assets and more significantly the related liabilities – taking them off balance sheet. UK Financial Reporting Standard (FRS) No 5 – Substance of Transactions aims to prevent assets and liabilities being taken off balance sheet. This Standard applies to all accounting and reporting, not just that of commercial companies. Thus anyone involved with PFI contracts must be aware of the issues involved.

IAS 17 does not address such issues, but any revision is likely to do so, possibly putting many PFI and the like loans back into government borrowings.

Objective and definitions from the Standard

Objective

The objective of this Standard is to prescribe, for lessees and lessors, the appropriate accounting policies and disclosure to apply in relation to finance and operating leases.

Definitions

A **lease** is an agreement whereby the lessor conveys to the lessee in return for a payment or a series of payments, the right to use an asset for an agreed period of time.

A **finance lease** is a lease that transfers substantially all the risks and rewards incident to ownership of an asset. Title may or may not eventually be transferred.

An **operating lease** is a lease other than a finance lease.

A **non-cancellable lease** is a lease that is cancellable only:

a) upon the occurrence of some remote contingency;

b) with the permission of the lessor;

c) if the lessee enters into a new lease for the same or an equivalent asset with the same lessor; or

d) upon payment by the lessee of an additional amount such that, at inception, continuation of the lease is reasonably certain.

The **inception of the lease** is the earlier of the date of the lease agreement, or of a commitment by the parties to the principal provisions of the lease.

The **lease term** is the non-cancellable period for which the lessee has contracted to lease the asset, together with any further terms for which the lessee has the option to continue to lease the asset, with or without further payment, which option at the inception of the lease it is reasonably certain that the lessee will exercise.

Minimum lease payments are the payments over the lease term that the lessee is, or can be, required to make excluding contingent rent, costs for services and taxes to be paid by and reimbursed to the lessor, together with:

a) in the case of the lessee, any amounts guaranteed by the lessee or by a party related to the lessee; or

b) in the case of the lessor, any residual value guaranteed to the lessor by either; the lessee, a party related to the lessee, or an independent third party financially capable of meeting this guarantee.

Fair value is the amount for which an asset could be exchanged or a liability settled between knowledgeable willing parties in an arm's length transaction.

Economic life is either:

a) the period over which the asset is expected to be economically useable by one or more users; or

b) the number of production or similar units expected to be obtained from the asset by one or more users.

Useful life is the estimated remaining period from the beginning of the lease term, without limitation by the lease term, over which the economic benefits embodied in the asset are expected to be consumed by the enterprise.

Guaranteed residual value is:

a) in the case of the lessee, that part of the residual value which is guaranteed by the lessee, or by a party related to the lessee (the amount of the guarantee being the maximum amount that could, in any event become payable); and

b) in the case of the lessor, that part of the residual value which is guaranteed by the lessee, or by a third party unrelated to the lessor who is financially capable of discharging the obligations under the guarantee.

Unguaranteed residual value is that portion of the residual value of the leased asset, the realisation of which by the lessor is not assured, or is guaranteed solely by a party related to the lessor.

Gross investment in the lease is the aggregate of the minimum lease payments under a finance lease from the standpoint of the lessor and any unguaranteed residual value accruing to the lessor.

Unearned finance income is the difference between:

a) the aggregate of the minimum lease payments under a finance lease from the standpoint of the lessor and any unguaranteed residual value accruing to the lessor; and

b) the present value of (a) above, at the interest rate implicit in the lease.

Net investment in the lease is the gross investment in the lease, less unearned financial income.

The **interest rate implicit in the lease** is the discount rate that, at the inception of the lease, causes the aggregate present value of (a) the minimum lease payment and (b) the unguaranteed residual value to be equal to the fair value of the asset.

The **lessee's incremental borrowing rate** of interest is the rate of interest the lessee would have to pay on a similar lease or, if that is not determinable, the rate that, at inception of the lease, the lessee would incur to borrow over a similar term, and with a similar security, the funds necessary to purchase the asset.

Contingent rent is that portion of the lease payments that is not fixed in amount but is based on a factor other than just the passage of time (e.g. percentage of sales, amount of usage, price indices, and market rates of interest).

Borrowing costs – IAS 23

Why needed

Borrowing costs related to the funding of revenue earning fixed assets are a recurring cost of operation and should be charged against the revenue earned.

But what about funding the construction of future revenue earning fixed assets?

A legitimate argument is that borrowing costs should be capitalized during the construction phase of a fixed asset. Unless clear rules exist, borrowing costs could disappear from the P&L account, instead appearing as a constituent of a fixed assets 'worth'! Capitalising revenue related costs was one of the techniques used by Worldcom to lower costs, and thus enhance earnings.

Ideas – concepts

Borrowing costs are an inevitable cost of funding business activities. They should most prudently be considered a cost to be charged as incurred against revenue.

However, fixed assets often require considerable funds to finance their construction or purchase. Borrowing costs incurred during the construction phase could legitimately be considered a necessary cost to bring the asset into a revenue earning condition, that is, they are a cost of the fixed asset as much as materials or labour are. A good way of justifying this view is to consider that if a business purchased a completed property say, the construction company that built the property would have factored into its selling price the borrowing costs of funding their work in progress during the property's construction.

Key terms

A qualifying asset is an asset that necessarily takes a substantial period of time to get ready for its intended use or sale.

Accounting

Borrowing costs should be recognized as an expense in the period in which they are incurred except to the extent that they are directly attributable to acquisition, construction or production of a qualifying asset.

Disclosure

The accounting policy adopted for borrowing costs should be disclosed. Also the amount of borrowing costs capitalized during the period and the interest rate used to determine the amount of capitalized borrowing costs.

Problem areas and questions to ask about the accounts

WHAT BORROWING COSTS QUALIFY TO BE CAPITALIZED?

Those that specifically relate to the construction of a fixed asset. An appropriate weighted average cost of relevant general borrowings may be capitalized.

CONSISTENCY OF APPROACH

If a policy of capitalizing interest is adopted then it must be applied to all qualifying assets – the policy cannot be used selectively. Businesses can either capitalize interest on all qualifying assets, or not apply it to any.

WHEN SHOULD CAPITALIZATION COMMENCE AND CEASE?

When expenditure and borrowing costs are being incurred on activities necessary to prepare the asset for its intended use. When all the preparatory activities are substantially complete then capitalization should cease.

WHAT HAPPENS IF A CAPITAL PROJECT IS SUSPENDED?

Capitalization should be suspended during extended periods during which active development is interrupted.

WHAT HAPPENS IF A PROJECT IS COMPLETED IN STAGES?

If each stage or part is capable of being used while construction continues on other parts, then capitalization of borrowing costs should cease for the part that is in revenue earning service.

Where the cost of assets contain an element of capitalized borrowing costs check that the asset is not over valued.

Key differences

There is no significant difference between the requirements of UK FRS 15 – Tangible Fixed Assets and this IAS.

Objective and definitions from the Standard

Objective

The objective of this Standard is to prescribe the accounting treatment for borrowing costs. This Standard generally requires the immediate expensing of borrowing costs. However, the Standard permits, as an allowed alternative treatment, the capitalisation of borrowing costs that are directly attributable to the acquisition, construction or production of a qualifying asset.

Definitions

Borrowing costs are interest and other costs incurred by an enterprise in connection with the borrowing of funds.

A **qualifying asset** is an asset that necessarily takes a substantial period of time to get ready for its intended use or sale.

Accounting for government grants and disclosure of government assistance – IAS 20

Why needed

There are different types of grant. Different names can also be used, e.g. subventions, subsidies etc. Grants may be given in support of either revenue or capital expenditure. Grants may also be unconditional or conditional upon achieving some target, e.g. numbers of people employed.

Without clear accounting rules the benefit of grants to businesses could be seriously miss-represented. For example, conditional grants given to support capital expenditure where the benefits accrue over the years of proper usage of the asset, could be credited directly to earnings in one year, without restriction.

Grants are given either as a contribution to revenue costs – e.g. 50% of the cost of wages reimbursed for a six month period to encourage employment, OR to encourage the investment in and use of assets – e.g. 40% of the cost of electronic equipment reimbursed.

It should be obvious that revenue grants are credited to the income statement as a reduction in the relevant cost, and capital grants are either credited as a reduction in the cost of the asset in the balance sheet, or held as a reserve to be released to the income statement as the relevant asset is consumed or depreciated.

However, without this Standard some might argue that capital grants are in effect income and thus credit the whole amount to the P&L account.

Ideas – concepts

The accruals concept requires that revenue and costs are accrued, that is, matched with one another so far as their relationship can be established or justifiably assumed. They are dealt with in the income statement of the period to which they relate.

Prudence means being cautious. Prudence is the inclusion of a degree of caution in the exercise of judgment needed in making the estimates required under conditions of uncertainty, such that assets or expenses are not overstated, and liabilities or expenses are not understated. Accordingly government grants should not be recognized in the income statement until the conditions for their receipt have been complied with and there is reasonable assurance that the grant will be received (and not be repayable to the provider).

Revenue grants that support a business by reducing running costs should be credited to earnings and the benefit in the accounting period affected should be disclosed.

Capital grants given to support purchase of fixed assets (infrastructure) that will benefit the business over the life of the assets, through a reduced charge for depreciation, should be shown as a liability and credited to the income statement as the asset is consumed – depreciated. Thus the benefit of the grant will be correctly matched with the use of the asset.

Any conditions attaching to grants, e.g. reaching certain production or employment targets, should be disclosed.

Key terms

Government assistance is action by government designed to provide an economic benefit specific to an enterprise or range of enterprises qualifying under certain criteria.

Government grants are assistance by government in the form of transfers of resources to an enterprise, in return for past or future compliance with certain conditions, relating to the operating activities of the enterprise.

Government refers to government, government agencies and similar bodies whether local, national or international, e.g. EU, World Bank or UN.

Accounting

Government grants should be recognized in the P&L account so as to match them with the expenditure towards which they are intended to contribute. Grants should not be recognized in the P&L until the conditions for receipt have been complied with.

Where a grant is made as a contribution towards expenditure on fixed assets then the grant should be treated as deferred income, credited to the P&L account by installments over the expected useful economic life of the related asset. The Standard also permits the cost of the fixed asset to be reduced by the amount of the grant – **this treatment is not permitted in the UK.**

Disclosure

The accounting policy adopted for government grants should be disclosed and the effect on the results for the period identified.

A note should be made of any unfulfilled conditions and other liabilities or contingencies attaching to the government assistance.

Problem areas and questions to ask about the accounts

CONDITIONAL GRANTS

Many grants are given on the basis that certain conditions are met. Until such times as these conditions are met the grants should be held as deferred income. Any release of a grant prior to clear compliance with conditions should only be done on a prudent basis.

GRANTS FOR IMMEDIATE FINANCIAL SUPPORT

A government grant that becomes receivable as compensation for expenses or losses already incurred, or for the purpose of giving immediate financial support with no future related costs, should be recognized as income when received – as a specifically disclosed (exceptional) item, if appropriate.

SIGNIFICANT DIFFERENCES IN GAAP

UK law does not permit the crediting of a grant to reduce the fixed asset cost.

Objective and definitions from the Standard

Objective

Note: there is no objective in IAS 20.

Government grants should be recognized in the income statement so as to match them with the expenditure towards which they are intended to contribute.

Definitions

Government refers to government, government agencies and similar bodies whether local, national or international.

Government assistance is action by government designed to provide an economic benefit specific to an enterprise or range of enterprises, qualifying under certain criteria. Government assistance for the purpose of this Standard does not include benefits provided only indirectly through action affecting general trading conditions, such as the provision of infrastructure in development areas, or the imposition of trading constraints on competitors.

Government grants are assistance by government in the form of transfers of resources to an enterprise in return for past or future compliance with certain conditions, relating to the operating activities of the enterprise. They exclude those forms of government assistance which cannot reasonably have a value placed upon them and transactions with government which cannot be distinguished from the normal trading transactions of the enterprise.

Grants related to assets are government grants whose primary condition is that an enterprise qualifying for them should purchase, construct or otherwise acquire long-term assets. Subsidiary conditions may also be attached restricting the type or location of the assets, or the periods during which they are to be acquired or held.

Grants related to income are government grants other than those related to assets.

Forgivable loans are loans which the lender undertakes to waive repayment of under certain prescribed conditions.

Fair value is the amount for which an asset could be exchanged between a knowledgeable willing buyer and a knowledgeable willing seller in an arm's length transaction.

Shared based payment – IFRS 2

Why needed

Entities often grant shares or share options to employees or other parties. Share option plans are a common feature of employee remuneration, for directors, senior executives and many other employees. Some entities issue shares or share options to pay suppliers, such as suppliers of professional services. Shareholders normally will have voted approval of such payment schemes, but with out calculation of the cost of the payment and full disclosure of long term effects such payments may appear 'free'. Awarding shares or share options means that a portion of the value of the company is being given away.

A stark example of the long term effect could be found in some US high tech companies who awarded staff with generous share options, the attraction to staff being the apparently limitless rise in the share price. The earnings per share -eps, being profit available for shareholders divided by the eligible number of shares could for example be 14 cents per share in respect of shares currently issued, but if all share options were exercised then the (diluted) eps figures could be as little as 6 cents per share. In effect the present owners could end up owning less than half of the company.

Ideas – concepts

The basic idea is to put a value on the cost of awarding share based payments and to recognize that cost immediately in profit and loss – there is no such thing as a free lunch!

Key terms

A share-based payment transaction is a transaction where an entity grants equity instruments (actual shares or share options) in consideration of the receipt of goods or services. Services could be employees working time.

A share based transaction can also be where an entity acquires goods or services by incurring liabilities to the supplier where the amount is based on the price of the entity's shares or other equity instruments of the entity.

An **equity-settled share-based payment transaction** is a share-based payment transaction in which the entity receives goods or services in exchange for equity instruments of the entity (including shares or share options).

A **cash-settled share-based payment transaction** is a share-based payment transaction in which the entity acquires goods or services by incurring a liability to transfer cash or other assets to the supplier of those goods or services for amounts that are based on the price (or value) of the entity's shares or other equity instruments of the entity.

Accounting

RECOGNITION

An entity should recognise the goods or services received or acquired in a share-based payment transaction when it obtains the goods or as the services are received. The entity shall recognise a corresponding increase in equity if the goods or services were received in an equity-settled share-based payment transaction, or a liability if the goods or services were acquired in a cash-settled share-based payment transaction. Goods or services received should be recognised as an expense or asset as appropriate.

EQUITY SETTLED SHARE BASED PAYMENT TRANSACTIONS

For equity-settled share-based payment transactions, the entity shall measure the goods or services received, and the corresponding increase in equity, directly, at the fair value of the goods or services received, unless that fair value cannot be estimated reliably. If the entity cannot estimate reliably the fair value of the goods or services received, the entity shall measure their value, and the corresponding increase in equity, indirectly, by reference to the fair value of the equity instruments granted.

The standard gives details of how to account for transactions in which services are received.

CASH SETTLED SHARE BASE TRANSACTIONS

The standard sets out the accounting for cash settled, share based with cash alternative and where there is a choice of settlement method.

DETERMINING THE FAIR VALUE OF EQUITY INSTRUMENTS GRANTED

For transactions measured by reference to the fair value of the equity instruments granted, an entity shall measure the fair value of equity instruments granted at the measurement *date*, based on market prices if available, taking into account the terms and conditions upon which those equity instruments were granted (subject to the requirements of paragraphs 19-22).

If market prices are not available, the entity shall estimate the fair value of the equity instruments granted using a valuation technique to estimate what the price of those equity instruments would have been on the measurement date in an arm's length transaction between knowledgeable, willing parties. The valuation technique shall be consistent with generally accepted valuation methodologies for pricing financial instruments, and shall incorporate all factors and assumptions that knowledgeable, willing market participants would consider in setting the price (subject to the requirements of paragraphs 19-22).

Disclosure

An entity shall disclose information that enables users of the financial statements to understand the nature and extent of share-based payment arrangements that existed during the period.

An entity shall disclose information that enables users of the financial statements to understand how the fair value of the goods or services received, or the fair value of the equity instruments granted, during the period was determined.

An entity shall disclose information that enables users of the financial statements to understand the effect of share-based payment transactions on the entity's profit or loss for the period and on its financial position

For each of the above disclosures there is a detailed list of specific disclosure requirements.

Problems areas and questions to ask about the accounts

DOES THE ISSUE OF SHARE OPTIONS FALL WITHIN THE SCOPE OF THE STANDARD?

As the standard is drafted to embrace most share based payments, it is very likely that the standard will apply.

ESTIMATING THE FAIR VALUE OF EQUITY INSTRUMENTS GRANTED

This was given as one of the barriers to the introduction of the standard. Appendix B of the standard outlines the issues and how apparent valuation difficulties may be overcome.

AMENDMENTS TO OTHER IFRSS

The adoption of this standard affects disclosure required by other standards. The principal standards affected are:

- **IAS 12 Income Taxes**. In some tax jurisdictions, an entity receives a tax deduction (ie an amount that is deductible in determining taxable profit) that relates to remuneration paid in shares, share options or other equity instruments of the entity. A deferred tax asset may arise. In some instances deferred tax should be recognised directly in equity

- In **IAS 16 Property, Plant and Equipment, IAS 38 Intangible Assets, and IAS 40 Investment Property**, the definition of cost is amended to read as follows:

  "Cost is the amount of cash or cash equivalents paid or the fair value of other consideration given to acquire an asset at the time of its acquisition or construction or, where applicable, the amount attributed to that asset when initially recognised in accordance with the specific requirements of other IFRSs, eg IFRS 2 Share-based Payment."

OTHER STANDARDS AFFECTED:

- IAS 19 Employee Benefits disclosure
- IAS 32 Financial Instruments: Disclosure and Presentation,
- IAS 33 Earnings per Share is amended as described below.
- IFRS 1First-time Adoption of International Financial Reporting Standards

Full details of the changes can be found in appendix C to IFRS2.

Objective and definitions from the standard

Objective

The objective of this IFRS is to specify the financial reporting by an entity when it undertakes a share-based payment transaction. In particular, it requires an entity to reflect in its profit or loss and financial position the effects of share-based payment transactions, including expenses associated with transactions in which share options are granted to employees.

Definitions

Cash-settled share-based payment transaction is a share-based payment transaction in which the entity acquires goods or services by incurring a liability to transfer cash or other assets to the supplier of those goods or services for amounts that are based on the price (or value) of the entity's shares or other equity instruments of the entity.

Employees and others providing similar services are individuals who render personal services to the entity and either:

a) the individuals are regarded as employees for legal or tax purposes,

b) the individuals work for the entity under its direction in the same way as individuals who are regarded as employees for legal or tax purposes, or

c) the services rendered are similar to those rendered by employees. For example, the term encompasses all management personnel, ie those persons having authority and responsibility for planning, directing and controlling the activities of the entity, including non-executive directors.

Equity instrument is a contract that evidences a residual interest in the assets of an entity after deducting all of its liabilities.

Equity instrument granted. The right (conditional or unconditional) to an equity instrument of the entity conferred by the entity on another party, under a share-based payment arrangement.

Equity-settled share-based payment transaction is a share-based payment transaction in which the entity receives goods or services as consideration for equity instruments of the entity (including shares or share options).

Fair value is the amount for which an asset could be exchanged, a liability settled, or an equity instrument granted could be exchanged, between knowledgeable, willing parties in an arm's length transaction.

Grant date is the date at which the entity and another party (including an employee) agree to a share-based payment arrangement, being when the entity and the counterparty have a shared understanding of the terms and conditions of the arrangement. At grant date the entity confers on the counterparty the right to cash, other assets, or equity instruments of the entity, provided the specified vesting conditions, if any, are met. If that agreement is subject to an approval process (for example, by shareholders), grant date is the date when that approval is obtained.

Intrinsic value is the difference between the fair value of the shares to which the counterparty has the (conditional or unconditional) right to subscribe or which it has the right to receive, and the price (if any) the counterparty is (or will be) required to pay for those shares. For example, a share option with an exercise price of CU15[1] on a share with a fair value of CU20, has an intrinsic value of CU5.

Market condition is a condition upon which the exercise price, vesting or exercisability of an equity instrument depends that is related to the market price of the entity's equity instruments, such as attaining a specified share price or a specified amount of intrinsic value of a share option, or achieving a specified target that is based on the market price of the entity's equity instruments relative to an index of market prices of equity instruments of other entities.

Measurement date is the date at which the fair value of the equity instruments granted is measured for the purposes of this IFRS. For transactions with employees and others providing similar services, the measurement date is grant date. For transactions with parties other than employees (and those providing similar services), the measurement date is the date the entity obtains the goods or the counterparty renders service.

---

1 In this appendix, monetary amounts are denominated in 'currency units' (CU).

Reload feature is a feature that provides for an automatic grant of additional share options whenever the option holder exercises previously granted options using the entity's shares, rather than cash, to satisfy the exercise price.

Reload option. A new share option granted when a share is used to satisfy the exercise price of a previous share option.

Share-based payment arrangement is an agreement between the entity and another party (including an employee) to enter into a share-based payment transaction, which thereby entitles the other party to receive cash or other assets of the entity for amounts that are based on the price of the entity's shares or other equity instruments of the entity, or to receive equity instruments of the entity, provided the specified vesting conditions, if any, are met.

Share-based payment transaction is a transaction in which the entity receives goods or services as consideration for equity instruments of the entity (including shares or share options), or acquires goods or services by incurring liabilities to the supplier of those goods or services for amounts that are based on the price of the entity's shares or other equity instruments of the entity.

Share option is a contract that gives the holder the right, but not the obligation, to subscribe to the entity's shares at a fixed or determinable price for a specified period of time.

Vest – to become an entitlement. Under a share-based payment arrangement, a counterparty's right to receive cash, other assets, or equity instruments of the entity vests upon satisfaction of any specified vesting conditions.

Vesting conditions are the conditions that must be satisfied for the counterparty to become entitled to receive cash, other assets or equity instruments of the entity, under a share-based payment arrangement. Vesting conditions include service conditions, which require the other party to complete a specified period of service, and performance conditions, which require specified performance targets to be met (such as a specified increase in the entity's profit over a specified period of time).

Vesting period is the period during which all the specified vesting conditions of a share-based payment arrangement are to be satisfied.

FIVE
Disclosure

5.1
Events after the balance sheet date – IAS 10

Why needed

Events may affect a company after the year end but before accounts are 'signed off'. Although these may not cause change to figures in the accounts **not** acknowledging their existence (by way of a note to the accounts) could be quite misleading.

Ideas – concepts

This obvious concept is that accounts should reflect all information available up to the date of sign off. If you obtain information that changes subjective views taken on figures in accounts after the balance sheet date, but before accounts are issued, then the account figures should be adjusted. These are *adjusting events.*

However, if some significant information is obtained, or event occurs that does not affect the historic figure shown in the financial statements but that will affect the current or future periods, then this should be reported. These are n*on adjusting events.* For example, a company's premises that are in the balance sheet at 1m at the year end date of 31 December, are burnt to the ground on 4 February of the following year – the premises did exist at the balance sheet date and were worth 1m – but not now! This significant fact should be disclosed.

Key terms

EVENTS AFTER THE BALANCE SHEET DATE OR POST BALANCE SHEET EVENTS

Post balance sheet events are those events, both favorable and unfavorable, which occur between the balance sheet date and the date on which the financial statements are approved by the board of directors – 'the date of sign off'.

ADJUSTING EVENTS

These are post balance sheet events that provide additional evidence of conditions existing at the balance sheet date. They include events which because of statutory or conventional requirements, are reflected in the financial statements.

NON-ADJUSTING EVENTS

These are post balance sheet events which concern conditions that did not exist at the balance sheet date.

Accounting

An enterprise should adjust the amounts recognized in its financial statements to reflect adjusting events after the balance sheet date

Disclosure

Financial statements should be prepared on the basis of conditions existing at the balance sheet date.

A material post balance sheet event should be disclosed where it is a non-adjusting event of such materiality that its non-disclosure would affect the ability of users of financial statements to reach a proper understanding of the financial position.

In determining which non-adjusting events are of sufficient materiality to require disclosure, regard should be had to all matters which are necessary to enable users of the financial statements to assess the financial position.

Problem areas and questions to ask about the accounts

DIVIDENDS

Dividends that are only proposed or declared after the balance sheet date should not be shown as a P&L charge with the corresponding liability shown in the balance sheet. Dividends are not really costs of a business, but rather appropriation of profits paid to equity shareholders. They should not be considered as provided for or accrued costs but can be disclosed either:

a) on the face of the balance sheet as a separate component of equity or

b) in the notes to the financial statements

DATE OF APPROVING AND SIGNING ACCOUNTS

Company law may clarify when financial statements are approved and 'finalized'. However, those involved in approving, and, more importantly signing financial statements, should be absolutely clear as to:

- when financial statements do become the final authorized version; and

- whether all post balance sheet events have been considered.

GOING CONCERN

The Standard reiterates the point that if there is any question at all that the company cannot continue as a going concern then this should be stated, and the financial statements adjusted accordingly.

Key differences

The Standard is uncontroversial and its requirements universally acknowledged.

Objective and definitions from the Standard

The objective of this Standard is to prescribe:

a) when an enterprise should adjust its financial statements for events after the balance sheet date; and

b) the disclosures that an enterprise should give about the date when the financial statements were authorized for issue and about events after the balance sheet date.

The Standard also requires that an enterprise should not prepare its financial statements on a going concern basis if events after the balance sheet date indicate that the going concern assumption is not appropriate.

Definitions

Events after the balance sheet date are those events, both favorable and unfavorable, that occur between the balance sheet date and the date when the financial statements are authorized for issue. Two types of events can be identified:

a) those that provide evidence of conditions that existed at the balance sheet date (adjusting events after the balance sheet date); and

b) those that are indicative of conditions that arose after the balance sheet date (non-adjusting events after the balance sheet date).

FURTHER UK DEFINITION

The date on which the financial statements are approved by the board of directors is the date the board of directors formally approve a set of documents as financial statements.

5.2
Related party disclosures – IAS 24

Why needed

Who really owns and controls the business?

Do owners (or their families) and those in authority and with power in the business, have personal deals with the business?

The above information is important if all those involved with the business are to be treated fairly.

Ideas – concepts

Users of accounts must know if any of those involved in running the business have 'interests' in the business. That is, do they have control to a greater or lesser degree over the business? Do they also either directly or though a close relationship have (favorable) dealings with the business?

Key terms

A **related party** is one where one party has the ability to control the other party or exercise significant influence over the other party.

A **related party transaction** is where there is or may be a transfer of resources or obligations between related parties.

Control is where by whatever means, a party has the ability to direct the financial and operating policies of the management of the enterprise.

Significant influence – participation in the financial and operating policy decisions of an enterprise, but not control of those policies.

Accounting

This Standard is all about disclosure.

Disclosure

Control – whether or not there have been transactions between the parties, details of who really controls the business should be disclosed. (Note: this requirement is applied with more rigour in the equivalent UK Standard.)

Transactions between related parties should be disclosed. The following are examples of the kinds of transaction that would require to be disclosed:

- Purchases and sales of property, goods and services.

- Agency and leasing agreements.

- Transfer of knowledge – R&D, licenses, patents etc.

- Finance, loans, guarantees etc.

- Management contracts.

Note: transactions of a similar nature may be aggregated, unless their separate disclosure is need for a true understanding of the financial statements.

Problem areas and questions to ask about the accounts

IDENTIFICATION OF RELATED PARTIES AND TRANSACTIONS

Identifying who really controls the business and who might be related parties may be difficult matters to establish. Do you know:

- Who really controls your business?

- What 'deals' the company has entered into with fellow executives?

How are transactions between related parties to be identified? The answer is to acknowledge the issue of possible related parties and have procedures in place. This would be part of corporate governance for public companies.

Key differences

The UK definition of and disclosure of, control is more rigorous than the IAS.

Objective and definitions from the Standard

Objective

The objective of this Standard is to prescribe the disclosure of information about related party relationships and about transactions and outstanding balances between an entity and its related parties.

Definitions

Related party – a party is a related party of an entity if:

a) directly, or indirectly through one or more intermediaries, it:

    i) controls, or is controlled by, or is under the common control with, the entity (this includes parents, subsidiaries and fellow subsidiaries)

    ii) has an interest in the equity that gives it significant influence over the entity; or

    iii) has joint control over the entity

b) it is an associate (as defined in IAS 28 Accounting for investments in Associates) of the entity;

c) it is a joint venture in which the entity is a venturer (see IAS 31 Financial Reporting of Interests in Joint Ventures);

d) it is a member of the key management personnel of the entity or its parent, that is, those persons having authority and responsibility for planning, directing and controlling the activities of the entity, directly or indirectly, including any director (whether executive or otherwise) or officer of that entity;

e) it is a close member of the family of any individual referred to in subparagraph a or d

f) it is an entity in which a controlling or jointly controlling interest in, or significant influence over, the voting power is owned, directly or indirectly, by any individual referred to in d or e above; or

g) it is a post employment benefit plan for the benefit of employees of the entity, or of any entity that is a related party of the entity

A related party transaction is a transfer of resources, services or obligations between related parties, regardless of whether a price is charged.

Control is the power to govern the financial and operating policies of an entity so as to obtain benefits from its activities.

Joint control is the contractually agreed sharing of control over an economic activity.

Significant influence – is the power to participation the financial and operating policy decisions of an entity, but is not control over those policies. Significant influence may be gained by share ownership, statute or agreement.

Close members of the family of an individual are those family members who may be expected to influence, or be influenced by, that individual in their dealings with the entity. They include:

a) the individual's domestic partner and children

b) children of the individual's domestic partner; and

c) dependents of the individual or the individual's domestic partner

Earnings per share – IAS 33

Why needed

Many businesses, investors and analysts see earnings per ordinary share (eps) as a prime measure of success (as long as it is increasing!). If there was no clear definition of what comprised 'earnings' the amount of earnings (profit) would be open to varying interpretations. Also it is possible to take differing views on the number of shares to be used in the denominator, e.g. should it be the number of shares in issue at the balance sheet date or the average number of shares in circulation during the year.

A further issue is that many companies have financial instruments, e.g. convertible loans, that if converted to ordinary shares would 'dilute' the eps figure.

Yet a more significant issue for some companies (e-businesses and high-tech businesses) is that share options have been granted to directors and managers. If all these options were to be exercised then the eps figures would be significantly lower or 'diluted'.

Ideas – concepts

Earnings per share is a measure of profitability. It is how much available profit, normally expressed in pence or cents, is generated per ordinary share issued. The idea is to show consistently among years and companies the profit attributable to each ordinary share owned. In a well managed company it would be expected that eps would increase year on year. Higher eps would allow higher dividends per share to be distributed. The projected growth of divided yield (per share) is an important figure when valuing shares.

Key terms

Earnings are the net profit or loss for the period attributable to ordinary shareholders. This is profit (or loss) after interest, taxation and any preference dividends. It is the profit that could potentially be paid out to ordinary shareholders as dividend.

The number of shares should be the weighted average number of ordinary shares outstanding during the period – NOT the number in issue at the year end or any other single date.

Diluted earnings are the earnings for the period after adjusting for the after tax effects of dividends, interest or any other changes in income or expense due to the effect of dilutive potential ordinary shares.

Diluted number of shares should be the weighted average number of ordinary shares, PLUS the weighted average number of potential ordinary shares – the potential shares are deemed to have been issued.

An **ordinary share** is an equity instrument that is subordinate to all other classes of equity instruments.

A **potential ordinary share** is a financial instrument or other contract that may entitle its holder to ordinary shares.

Examples of potential ordinary shares are:

a) debt or equity instruments, including preferences shares, that are convertible into ordinary shares;

b) share warrants and options;

c) rights granted under employee share plans that may entitle employees to receive ordinary shares as part of their remuneration and similar rights granted under other share purchase plans; and

e) rights to ordinary shares that are contingent upon the satisfaction of certain conditions resulting from contractual arrangements, such as the purchase of a business or other assets, i.e. contingently issuable shares.

Warrants or options are financial instruments that give the holder the right to purchase ordinary shares.

Accounting

Measurement or numbers to be used:

(BASIC) EARNINGS PER SHARE

Basic earnings per share should be calculated by dividing the net profit or loss for the period attributable to ordinary shareholders, by the weighted average number of ordinary shares outstanding during the period.

DILUTED EARNINGS PER SHARE

For the purpose of calculating diluted earnings per share, the net profit attributable to ordinary shareholders and the weighted average number of shares outstanding should be adjusted of the effects of all dilutive potential ordinary shares.

RESTATEMENT

If the number or ordinary or potential ordinary shares increases as a result of capitalisation, bonus issue, share split or other reasons, the calculation of earnings per share (and diluted eps) should be re-calculated retrospectively.

Disclosure

Basic and diluted earnings per share should be presented, with equal prominence, on the face of the income statement.

If an enterprise discloses additional eps figures, e.g. excluding a one off, exceptional cost, then the calculations should be as for basic or diluted eps figures. All eps figures should be disclosed with equal prominence.

An enterprise should disclose:

- the amounts used as the numerators for any eps figures and a reconciliation of the amounts to the reported net profit or loss for the period; and
- the weighted average numbers of ordinary shares used as the denominator of any eps figure. A reconciliation among the differing numbers of ordinary shares should be given where appropriate.

Problem areas and questions to ask about the accounts

CHANGES IN NUMBER OF SHARES IN ISSUE DURING THE YEAR

Ordinary shares may be issued or the number reduced without any change in resources. Examples include: share splits, capitalization of a bonus issue of shares (a stock dividend). In such cases the weighted average number of ordinary shares should be adjusted for such events.

WHERE DEEMED DILUTION INCREASES EPS

Potential ordinary shares should be treated as dilutive when, and only when, their conversion to ordinary shares would decrease net profit per share from continuing ordinary operations.

This constraint is presumably to prevent some clever manipulation of financial instruments that would give rise to an apparent increase in eps.

Objective and definitions from the Standard

Objective

The objective of this Standard is to prescribe principles for the determination and presentation of earnings per share for profit or loss from continuing operations and for net profit or loss for the period (each for the amount attributable to ordinary shareholders), so as to improve performance comparisons among different enterprises in the same period and among different accounting periods for the same entity. Even though earnings per share data have limitations because of different accounting policies that may be used for determining 'earnings', a consistently determined denominator enhances financial reporting. The focus of this Standard is on the denominator of the earnings per share calculation.

Definitions

An **ordinary share** is an equity instrument that is subordinate to all other classes of equity instruments.

A **potential ordinary share** is a financial instrument or other contract that may entitle its holder to ordinary shares.

Warrants or options are financial instruments that give the holder the right to purchase ordinary shares.

Contingently issuable ordinary shares are ordinary shares issuable for little or no cash or other consideration upon satisfaction of certain conditions pursuant to a contingent share agreement.

Dilution is a reduction in earnings per share or an increase in loss per share resulting from the assumption that convertible securities were converted, that options or warrants were exercised, or that ordinary shares were issued upon the satisfaction of certain conditions.

Financial instruments: Disclosure and presentation – IAS 32

Why needed

What is debt (loans) and what is equity (risk capital)? It should be obvious, but with today's fashion, pressure and genuine need for diverse financial instruments it may be that the distinction is not clear. This Standard aims to define what is not equity.

A business may have borrowings and loans – definite liabilities, but can also have entered into and committed itself to further liabilities by dint of entering options and other contracts. The aim (or hope might be a better word) is to make gains or at least balance gains and losses. The issue is to what is the extent of these, often 'off balance sheet' liabilities. Also are there corresponding assets to support the liabilities?

The aim is to give information that can help identify the risks a business has in respect of financial instruments

Ideas – concepts

EQUITY OR LIABILITY?

Equity is 'free', i.e. does not have to pay interest, although shareholders do expect a return – dividends and/or capital growth. Equity (risk capital) is last in line for repayment on liquidation. Loans are liabilities – an obligation to transfer economic benefits as a result of past transactions or events (usually receipt of cash when the load is granted). Thus loans are a clear liability and also require interest to be paid – an expense.

The correct classification is vital – just what are business liabilities?

SPECULATIVE TRANSACTIONS

A derivative is a financial instrument whose value depends on the values of other, more basic underlying variables. Commonly these variables are the prices of traded assets – shares, oil or currencies. The issue here is that there may be no liability at present and the hope is that the transactions entered into will yield a gain. But there may be significant potential losses.

Full details of such transactions should be disclosed along with the reasons for using such financial instruments.

HEDGING

Hedging (as in hedge your bets) means having matched assets and liabilities where the change in the value of one will be covered, or off-set, by a compensating change in the other's value.

A common use of hedging is where investments are made in one currency and the financing is obtained in the same currency, or a currency that is linked to the currency of the investment – if the value of the investment falls, then the amount of financing to be repaid falls by an equal amount. However, businesses may also speculate on currency movements. There may be an unrelated compensating asset or liability, but there is no true hedge in this case.

Key terms

A **financial instrument** is any contract that gives rise to both a financial asset of one enterprise and a financial liability or equity instrument of another enterprise.

Note: commodity contracts are also financial instruments unless the commodity contracts are those of a normally functioning commodity trading company.

An **equity instrument** is any contract that evidences a residual interest in the assets of an enterprise after deducting all of its liabilities.

Derivative financial instrument is a financial instrument that delivers its value from the price or rate of some underlying item.

A **financial liability** is any liability that is a contractual obligation to deliver cash or another financial asset to another enterprise, or to exchange financial instruments with another enterprise under conditions that are potentially unfavorable.

A **financial asset** is any asset that is a contractual right to receive cash or another financial asset from another enterprise; a contractual right to exchange financial instruments with another enterprise under conditions that are potentially favorable; or an equity instrument of another enterprise.

Accounting

CLASSIFICATION

A financial instrument should be correctly classified as a liability or equity using the definitions in the Standard. The critical distinction is that equity will NOT have a contractual obligation to either deliver cash or another financial asset to another party. If a financial instrument contains both equity and liability then the component parts should be disclosed separately.

Interest, dividends or loses and gains, on financial instruments should be disclosed in the income statement. Dividends on equity instruments should be debited against equity – they are not an expense of the business, but rather a distribution of equity.

OFF-SETTING

Financial assets and liabilities should be off-set where there is a right of off-set and the enterprise intends to settle on a net basis, or realize the asset and settle the liability simultaneously.

Disclosure

This Standard is really focused on disclosure of all aspects of an enterprise's dealing in financial instruments. If there is full disclosure of all pertinent facts then readers of financial statements will be better able to assess risk and the potential financial stability (or nor) of the enterprise.

RISK MANAGEMENT POLICIES

An enterprise should describe its financial risk management objectives and policies.

ACCOUNTING POLICIES, TERMS AND CONDITIONS

The accounting policies adopted for financial instruments along with details of significant terms and conditions that may affect the amount, timing and certainty of future cash flows should be disclosed.

INTEREST RATE RISK

For each class of financial asset and liability an enterprise should disclose information about its exposure to interest rate risk – details of maturity dates, rates etc.

CREDIT RISK

For each class of financial asset an enterprise should disclose information about its exposure to credit risk – risk of bad debts. This should include its likely maximum exposure and note any concentration of potential bad debts.

FAIR VALUE

For each class of financial asset and financial liability, both recognized and unrecognized, an enterprise should disclose information about fair value.

Note: with the adoption of IAS 39 – Financial Instruments: Recognition and Measurement many financial assets and financial liabilities will have to be revalued to fair value. However, disclosure of facts relating to fair value valuations must still be required.

DISCLOSURE WHEN ASSETS ARE CARRIED AT AN AMOUNT IN EXCESS OF THEIR FAIR VALUE

When an enterprise carries financial assets at amounts in excess of their fair value, the carrying amount (estimate) of fair value should be disclosed along with the reason for not reducing the asset's carrying amount to fair value.

Problem areas and questions to ask about the accounts

AMOUNT OF DATA

Appendix A of the Standard gives examples on how to apply the Standard. Undoubtedly there is potentially a huge amount of data to be assembled and disclosed. If IAS's are being adopted for the first time then it is important not to underestimate the time it will take to ensure compliance with this Standard.

COMPLETENESS

Have all financial assets and liabilities been identified?

Objective and definitions from the Standard

Objective

The dynamic nature of international financial markets has resulted in the widespread use of a variety of financial instruments, ranging from traditional primary instruments, such as bonds, to various forms of derivative instruments such as interest rate swaps. The objective of this Standard is to enhance financial statement users' understanding of the significance of on the balances sheet and off balance sheet financial instruments, to an enterprise's financial position, performance and cash flows.

The Standard prescribes certain requirements for presentation of on-the-balance sheet financial instruments and identifies information that should be disclosed about both on the balance sheet (recognized) and off-the-balance sheet (unrecognized) financial instruments. The presentation standards deal with the classification of related instruments between liabilities and equity, the classification of related interest, dividends, losses and gains, and the circumstances in which financial assets and liabilities should be offset. The disclosure standards deal with information about factors that affect the amount, timing and certainty of an enterprise's future cash flows relating to financial instruments and the accounting policies applied to the instruments. In addition the Standard encourages disclosure of information about the nature and extent of an enterprise's use of financial instruments, the business purposes that they serve, the risks associated with them and management's policies for controlling those risks.

Definitions

A **financial instrument** is any contract that gives rise to both a financial asset of one enterprise and a financial liability or equity instrument of another enterprise.

Commodity based contracts that give either party the right to settle in cash or some other financial instrument should be accounted for as if they were financial instruments, with the exception of commodity contracts that (a) were entered into and continue to meet the enterprise's expected purchase, sale, or usage requirements, (b) were designated for that purpose at their inception, and (c) are expected to be settled by delivery.

A **financial asset** is any asset that is:

a) cash;

b) a contractual right to receive cash or another financial asset from another enterprise;

c) a contractual right to exchange financial instruments with another enterprise under conditions that are potentially favorable; or

d) an equity instrument of another enterprise.

A **financial liability** is any liability that is a contractual obligation:

a) to deliver cash or another financial asset to another enterprise; or

b) to exchange financial instruments with another enterprise under conditions that are potentially unfavorable.

An **equity instrument** is any contract that evidences a residual interest in the assets of an enterprise after deducting all of its liabilities.

Monetary financial assets and financial liabilities (also referred to as monetary financial instruments) are financial assets and financial liabilities to be received, or paid in fixed or determinable amounts of money.

Fair value is the amount for which an asset could be exchanged or a liability settled between knowledgeable, willing parties in an arm's length transaction.

Market value is the amount obtainable from the sale, or payable on the acquisition, of a financial instrument in an active market.

5.5

Financial Instruments: Recognition and measurement – IAS 39

Why needed

A business may have borrowings and loans – clear liabilities, but can have entered into and committed itself to further huge liabilities by dint of entering options and other contracts – with the hope of gaining, or at least managing, the potential for losses – BUT where are the assets to support gains? AND what is the extent of the possible liabilities?

This Standard is the follow on to IAS 32, Financial Instruments: Disclosure and Presentation, and aims to quantify, or at least reveal in monetary terms, the effect of owning financial assets and being committed to financial liabilities. This is a very controversial Standard and a revised version is due to be issued in due course.

Ideas – concepts

VALUATION OF FINANCIAL ASSETS AND LIABILITIES

Financial assets – investments and loans are unlikely to hold a constant value over time. The very word 'investment' implies that there is an expectation of income or profit. This income or profit may be paid over periodically or subsumed in the original investment, and thus increase its value. Financial assets may also lose value. The concept of writing down assets to their realizable amount is well established – the prudence concept. However, there are many possible bases for valuing assets that appreciate in value. The most prudent is to leave them at original cost, thus understating balance sheet value. As outlined in the introduction a driving principal of the Standards is to make the balance sheet more of a valuation statement. This Standard thus requires financial assets to be shown at fair value in the balance sheet and any resultant profit or loss on revaluation shown in the income statement or against equity, where appropriate.

HEDGING

Hedging means having matched assets and liabilities where the change in the value of one will be covered or off-set by a compensating change in the other's value.

A common use of hedging is where investments are made in one currency and the financing is obtained in the same currency, or a currency that is linked to the currency of the investment – if the value of the investment falls, then the amount of financing to be repaid falls by an equal amount. However, businesses may also speculate on currency movements. There may be an unrelated compensating asset or liability, but there is no true hedge in this case. The Standard aims to allow hedge accounting only where hedging genuinely exists.

Key terms

A **financial instrument** is any contract that gives rise to both a financial asset of one enterprise and a financial liability or equity instrument, of another enterprise.

A **financial liability** is any liability that is a contractual obligation to deliver cash/financial asset to another enterprise or to exchange financial instruments with another enterprise, under conditions that are potentially unfavourable.

An **equity instrument** is any contract that evidences a residual interest in the assets of an enterprise after deducting all of its liabilities.

Fair value is the amount for which an asset could be exchanged between knowledgeable, willing parties in an arm's length transaction.

Hedging means designating one or more hedging item (e.g. an asset held for hedging purposes) so that their change in fair value is an off-set, in whole or part, to the change in fair value or cash flows of another hedged item (a liability held for hedging purposes).

A **derivative** is a financial instrument whose value depends on the values of other, more basic underlying variables. Commonly these variables are the prices of traded assets – shares, oil or currencies.

An **embedded derivative** is a component of a combined or hybrid financial instrument that has both a host contract and the (embedded) derivative – the effect is that the cash flows of the combined derivative vary in a way similar to a stand-alone derivative.

Accounting

All financial assets and financial liabilities should be recognized on the balance sheet, including all derivatives.

INITIAL RECOGNITION

An enterprise should recognize a financial asset or financial liability in its balance sheet when, and only when, it becomes a party to the contractual provisions of the instrument. Both financial assets and financial liabilities should initially be recognized at cost – the fair value of the consideration given or received to acquire the asset or liability.

SUBSEQUENT TO INITIAL RECOGNITION – FINANCIAL ASSETS

Financial assets should be re-measured to fair value except for:

a) loans and receivables originated by the enterprise and not held for trading purposes; e.g. debtors or a loan made to a supplier

b) fixed maturity investments that the enterprise will hold to maturity; and

c) financial assets whose fair value cannot be readily measured, e.g. shares in a private company.

Note: such cases are seen as uncommon, e.g. some equity instruments with no quoted market price.

Financial assets under a, b or c should be carried at amortized cost but also reviewed for impairment.

SUBSEQUENT TO INITIAL RECOGNITION – FINANCIAL LIABILITIES

After acquisition, most financial liabilities should be measured at original recorded amount, less repayments of principal. Only derivatives and liabilities held for trading should be re-measured to fair value.

RECOGNITION OF ADJUSTMENTS TO FAIR VALUE

Adjustments to fair value may be either:

a) recognized as a component of the net profit or loss for the period; or

b) only those changes in fair value relating to trading need be recognized as a component of profit or loss, other value changes being reported as changes in equity until such time as the financial asset is sold and a realized gain or loss then reported as a component of profit or loss.

Hedge accounting is permitted under this Standard in certain circumstances, provided that the hedging relationship is clearly defined, measurable, and actually effective.

Disclosure

Financial statements should include all the disclosures required by IAS 32 – Financial Instruments: Disclosure and Presentation, except that fair value disclosures are not applicable to those financial assets and liabilities that are now carried at fair value under this Standard.

The following should be included in the disclosures:

a) Methods and significant assumptions in estimating fair values.

b) Where gains and losses from changes in fair value have been recognised – in the profit or loss for the period or against equity.

Note: The Standard has further specific and detailed disclosure requirements for many types of financial instrument.

DISCLOSURES – HEDGING ACTIVITIES

a) A description of the enterprise's risk management objectives and policies – each type of hedge activity.

b) For each type of hedge – fair value/cash flow/net investment in a foreign entity:

  i) a description of the hedge

  ii) the financial instruments involved in the hedge

  iii) the nature of the risks being hedged

  iv) details where forecasts are used

c) Where cash flow hedge gains or losses have been recognised directly in equity, details of the movements.

Problem areas and questions to ask about the accounts

USE OF FAIR VALUES

The Standard's requirement that financial assets and liabilities (apart from genuine hedging situations and where financial assets or liabilities are to be held to maturity) should be revalued to fair value at each balance sheet date, is the main objection of many to the Standard. They, maybe rightly, argue that the financial assets and liabilities that they hold are part of a longer term, dynamic portfolio of net investment – the values should not just be viewed on one particular day. They argue too, again rightly, that the requirement to revalue to fair value each year will probably give rise to wide fluctuations in balance sheet values and net income.

But to ignore values altogether and wait until settlement of financial assets and liabilities may hide, or at least ignore, some nasty (or possibly positive) surprises.

Objective and definitions from the Standard

Objective

The objective of this Standard is to establish principles for recognising, measuring and disclosing information about financial instruments in the financial statements of business enterprises.

Definitions

A **financial instrument** is any contract that gives rise to both a financial asset of one enterprise and a financial liability, or equity instrument of another enterprise.

A **financial asset** is any asset that is:

a) cash;

b) a contractual right to receive cash or another financial asset from another enterprise;

c) a contractual right to exchange financial instruments with another enterprise under conditions that are potentially favourable; or

d) an equity instrument of another enterprise.

A **financial liability** is any liability that is a contractual obligation:

a) to deliver cash or another financial asset to another enterprise; or

b) to exchange financial instruments with another enterprise under conditions that are potentially unfavourable.

An **equity instrument** is any contract that evidences a residual interest in the assets of an enterprise after deducting all of its liabilities.

Fair value is the amount for which an asset could be exchanged between knowledgeable, willing parties in an arm's length transaction.

A **derivative** is a financial instrument:

a) whose value changes in response to the change in a specified interest rate, security price, commodity price, foreign exchange rate, index of prices or rates, a credit rating or credit index, or similar variable (sometimes called the 'underlying');

b) that requires no initial net investment or little initial net investment relative to other types of contracts that have a similar response to changes in market conditions; and

c) is settled at a future date.

A **financial asset or liability held for trading** is one that was acquired or incurred principally for the purpose of generating a profit from short-term fluctuations in price or dealer's margin.

Held to maturity investments are financial assets with fixed or determinable payments and fixed maturity that an enterprise has the positive intent and ability to hold to maturity.

Loans and receivables originated by the enterprise are financial assets that are created by the enterprise by providing money, goods or services directly to a debtor, other than those that are originated with the intent to be sold immediately or in the short term, which should be classified as held for trading.

Available-for-sale financial assets are those financial assets that are not loans and receivables originated by the enterprise, not held-to-maturity investments nor financial assets held for trading.

Amortised cost of a financial asset or financial liability is the amount at which the financial asset or liability was measured at initial recognition, minus principal repayments, plus or minus the cumulative amortisation of any difference between that additional amount and the maturity amount, and minus any write down for impairment or uncollectability.

The **effective interest rate method** is a method of calculating an amortisation using the effective interest rate of a financial asset or financial liability.

The **effective interest rate** is the rate that exactly discounts the expected stream of future cash payments through maturity or the next market-based re-pricing date to the current net carrying amount of the financial asset or liability.

Transaction costs are incremental costs that are directly attributable to the acquisition or disposal of a financial asset or liability.

A **firm commitment** is a binding agreement for the exchange of a specified quantity of resources at a specified price on a specified future date or dates.

Control of an asset is the power to obtain the future economic benefits that flow from the asset.

De-recognising means to remove a financial asset or liability, or a portion of a financial asset or liability, from an enterprise's balance sheet.

DEFINITIONS RELATING TO HEDGE ACCOUNTING

Hedging, for accounting purposes, means designating one or more hedging instruments so that their change in fair value is an off-set, in whole or part, to the change in fair value or cash flows of a hedged item.

A **hedged item** is an asset, liability, firm commitment, or forecasted future transaction that (a) exposes the enterprise to risk of changes in fair value or changes in future cash flows and that (b) for hedge accounting purposes, is designated as being hedged.

A **hedging instrument**, for hedge accounting purposes, is a designated derivative or (in limited circumstances) another financial asset or liability whose fair value or cash flows are expected to offset changes in the fair value or cash flows of a designated hedged item.

Hedge effectiveness is the degree to which offsetting changes in fair value or cash flows attributable to a hedged risk are achieved by the hedging instrument.

Securitisation is the process by which financial assets are transformed into securities.

SIX

Accounting for groups and investments

6.1

Business combinations – IFRS 3

Why needed

The majority of business combinations are the result of one entity bidding for and taking over another entity – one entity purchases another.

This standard requires all business combinations to be accounted for by applying the purchase method – acquisition accounting. The Standard setters require that an acquirer be identified – they state that there is no such thing as a merger or combining of interests.

Acquired assets should be disclosed at "fair value" on acquisition and any goodwill arising recognised as an asset in the balance sheet. Goodwill is to remain in the balance sheet at cost subject to any write down required as a result of a normally annual test for impairment.

Acquisition accounting is the one acceptable method.

> **NOTE**: after businesses combine consolidated or group financial statements will have to be prepared. The accounting and disclosure required for group accounts is covered by IAS 27 – Consolidated and Separate Financial Statements.

A simple example of consolidation is shown in chapter x pages x to x.

It is feasible that two businesses could combine their interests and merge. So why do the Standard setters deny the possibility? Merger accounting allows net assets to be combined at their (historical) values as per individual companies' accounts. Since neither takes over the other no revision of the combined assets to fair value is needed and no goodwill arises. The combined business balance sheet is likely to have out of date and understated net assets – this offends the Standard setters. Pooling of interests or merger accounting has for some time not been permitted in the US, Australia and other countries, and thus an important reason for the issuing of this standard is to achieve convergence.

Ideas – concepts

ACQUISITION ACCOUNTING AND GOODWILL

The concept is that there will always be one company taking over another. Fair values should be assigned to the acquired company's assets and any premium paid above this amount is goodwill arising on acquisition. This goodwill is an asset that as been paid for either with cash or by share issue. Goodwill is the generic term. Specific examples of what underlies goodwill are trade names, brands, patents, customer base and know how, or a good management team. The Standard requires that goodwill is shown as an asset and any write downs (impairments) are charged to the income statement. This standard is one of several that pursue the move to make balance sheets more valuation statements – balance sheets with more up to date values.

The previous version of this Standard suggested 20 years as a reasonable period over which to amortise (depreciate – write off) goodwill. This was really rather arbitrary and this revision takes the more sensible view that goodwill should be reviewed each year (or more frequently, if need be) for impairment (see IAS 36). Thus goodwill will remain in the balance sheet at cost. This implies that the name, brand, patents or whatever constituted the goodwill will be supported, by say advertising or development costs.

Whilst this is an improvement on previous practice it still does not permit calculation and recognition of appreciation in the value of goodwill – are the Standard setters being too prudent or are they preventing the opening of a Pandora's box of spurious revaluations? Goodwill is the most elusive of all business assets. Ask Arthur Andersen!

Mergers

If merger accounting was allowed the combined business balance sheet would have out of date and understated net assets – this offends the Standard setters. Another argument in favour of disallowing merger accounting is the fact that there are probably very few cases, at least of listed companies, where there is a true merger. There will always be a "take-over" of one business by the other.

Key terms

An **acquisition** is a business combination in which one of the entities, the acquirer, obtains control over the net assets and operations of another entity, the acquiree, in exchange for the transfer of assets, incurrence of liability or issue of equity.

A **uniting of interests or merger** is a business combination in which the shareholders of the combining enterprises combine control over the whole, or effectively the whole, of their net assets and operations to achieve a continuing mutual sharing in the risks and benefits attaching to the combined equity such that neither party can be identified as the acquirer.

NOTE: a simple example of consolidation is shown in chapter x pages x to x.

Accounting

All business combinations shall be accounted for by applying the purchase (acquisition) method. Thus an acquirer (the entity in control) will have to be identified for all business combinations

An acquisition of one business by another should be accounted for by the cost (being the aggregate of assets given, typically cash, shares etc, and any other directly attributable costs) being matched with the fair value of the assets and liabilities of the acquired business. Any excess of cost over fair value acquired is goodwill. Negative goodwill arises if the fair values exceed the cost of acquisition or price paid.

The standard sets out detailed requirements for allocating the cost of a business combination to the acquired assets, liabilities and contingent liabilities.

Fair values will be applied to all the assets and liabilities of the acquired company, even where there is a minority interest in the acquired company.

Goodwill

At the acquisition date the goodwill will be recognised as an asset at cost, being the excess of the fair value of net assets acquired less the cost of the acquisition.

Subsequently the acquirer shall measure goodwill at cost less any accumulated impairment loss.

Excess of acquirer's interest in the acquired entities net fair value over cost.

If the price paid for an acquisition is less than the fair value of the net assets acquired then there will be negative goodwill or a 'capital reserve'. The standard requires that the identification and measurement of the net assets acquired is reassessed (why would someone sell you something on the cheap!) If the valuation are correct then any surplus should be recognised immediately in profit and loss.

TRANSITIONAL PROVISIONS

As the change from amortising good will to carrying it at cost (cost less impairment) is significant the standard sets out guidance for the treatment of previously recognised good will.

Disclosure

The following should be disclosed:

a) Information that enables users of an entity's financial statements to evaluate the nature and financial effect of business combinations that have been completed by the balance sheet date or after the balance sheet date but before the financial statements were authorised for issue. Specific information is outlined in the standard but will include the names of the parties involved, acquisition date etc.

b) Information that enables users of an entity's financial statements to evaluate the financial effect of gains, losses or other adjustments recognised in the current period that relate to business combinations.

c) Information that enables users of an entity's financial statements to evaluate changes in the carrying amount of good will during the period.

Problems areas and questions to ask about the accounts

DATE OF ACQUISITION

An issue can be – from what date should sales and income be incorporated into consolidated accounts. The Standard defines the effective date of acquisition.

COST OF A BUSINESS CONTINGENT ON FUTURE EVENTS

The standard sets out that the cost of an acquisition should include

the increase or decrease that may occur from a probable contingent event, eg where it is probable that the price paid will be adjusted if sales do not reach some target. The standard defines 'probable'.

ASCERTAINING FAIR VALUES

"Fair value" is often subjective. The Standard reiterates that assets and liabilities should only be recognised where economic benefits flow to or from the enterprise and they can be reliably measured.

INTANGIBLE ASSETS

The standard requires the valuation and disclosure of any identifiable intangibles – eg an in-process development project that is successfully underway. Simply identifying one total figures of 'goodwill' will not be adequate.

Any intangible asset identified does have to meet the definition found in IAS 38 Intangible Assets and its fair value must be capable of being measured reliably.

IAS 38 gives guidance on these issues and is crossed referred to on this standard.

PROVISIONS

One way of suppressing results would be to provide, say for, rationalisation of the combined business activities. Since the extent of such costs may be highly subjective it would be easy to over-provide (bad news today) and then release the (un-needed) provision in future periods. The Standard demands that a rigorous approach be taken when identify amounts to be provided.

DIFFERENCES IN GAAP

Over the years there has been considerable harmonisation between UK, US and IAS practice. This standard brings accounting for business combinations into line with US and other countries standard setters. Differences may remain are in areas of: what constitutes a group and publication requirements.

Objective and definitions from the standard

Objective

The objective of this IFRS is to specify the financial reporting by an entity when it undertakes a business combination. In particular it specifies that all business combinations should be accounted for by applying the purchase method. Therefore, the acquirer recognises the acquiree's identifiable assets, liabilities and contingent liabilities at their fair values at the acquisition date, and also recognises goodwill, which is subsequently tested for impairment rather than amortised.

Definitions

Acquisition date is the date on which the acquirer effectively gains control of the acquiree.

Agreement date is the date that a substantive agreement between the combining parties is reached and, in the case of publicly listed entities, announced to the public. In the case of a hostile takeover, the earliest date that a substantive agreement between the combining parties is reached is the date that a sufficient number of the acquiree's owners have accepted the acquirer's offer for the acquirer to obtain control of the acquiree.

Business is an integrated set of activities and assets conducted and managed for the purpose of providing:

a) a return to investors; or

b) lower costs or other economic benefits directly and proportionately to policyholders or participants

A business generally consists of inputs, processes applied to those inputs, and resulting outputs that are, or will be, used to generate revenues. If goodwill is present in a transferred set of activities and assets, the transferred set shall be presumed to be a business.

A **business combination** is the bringing together of separate entities or businesses into one reporting entity.

Business combinations involving entities or businesses under common control are business combinations in which all of the combining entities or businesses ultimately are controlled by the same party or parties both before and after the combination, and that control is not transitory.

A contingent liability has the meaning given to it in IAS 37 Provisions, Contingent liabilities and contingent assets:

a) a possible obligation that arises from past events and whose existence will be confirmed by the occurrence or non-occurrence of one or more uncertain future events not wholly within the control of the enterprise; or

b) a present obligation that arises from past events but is not recognised because:

   i   it is not probable that an outflow of resources embodying economic benefits will be required to settle the obligation; or

   ii   the amount of the obligation cannot be measured with sufficient reliability

Control is the power to govern the financial and operating policies of an enterprise so as to obtain benefits from its activities.

Date of exchange When a business combination is achieved in a single exchange transaction, the date of exchange is the acquisition date. When a business combination involves more than one exchange transaction, for example when it is achieved in stages by successive share purchases, the date of exchange is the date that each individual investment is recognised in the financial statements of the acquirer.

Fair value is the amount for which an asset could be exchanged, or a liability settled, between knowledgeable, willing parties in an arm's length transaction.

Goodwill is future economic benefit arising from assets that are not capable of being individually identified and separately recognised.

An intangible asset has the meaning given to it in IAS 38 Intangible Assets, ie an identifiable non-monetary asset without physical substance.

A joint venture has the meaning given to it in IAS 31 Interests in Joint Ventures, ie a contractual arrangement whereby two or more parties undertake an economic activity that is subject to joint control.

A minority interest is that portion of the profit or loss and net assets of a subsidiary attributable to equity interests that are not owned, directly or indirectly through subsidiaries, by the parent.

Mutual entity is a entity other than an investor-owned entity, such as a mutual insurance company or a mutual cooperative entity, that provides lower costs or other economic benefits directly and proportionately to its policyholders or participants.

A parent is a entity that has one or more subsidiaries.

Probable means more likely than not.

A reporting entity is an entity for which there are users who rely on the entity's general purpose financial statements for information that will be useful to them for making decisions about the allocation of resources. A reporting entity can be a single entity or a group comprising a parent and all of its subsidiaries.

A subsidiary is an entity, including an unincorporated entity such as a partnership, that is controlled by another entity (known as the parent).

6.2

Consolidated and separate financial statements – IAS 27

Why needed

To understand a group of company's performance it is the total results and net assets of the group that is important. In the UK, as in most countries, company law requires that groups of companies produce group or consolidated accounts.

Concepts

The results and net assets of a group of companies could be reported by sending shareholders a set of the parent and subsidiary companies' accounts. This would NOT be very helpful. The concept of consolidation is that the sales, costs, assets, liabilities and cash flows of the parent and subsidiaries, are combined or consolidated (eliminating any inter company transactions and balances) to give the overall position in the income statement (P&L account), balance sheet and cash flows statement.

Note: a simple example of consolidation is shown in chapter 9.4.

Key terms

CONSOLIDATION

The process of adjusting and combining financial information from individual financial statements of a parent undertaking and its subsidiary undertaking, to prepare consolidated financial statements that present financial information for the group as a single economic entity.

CONTROL

The ability of an undertaking to direct the financial and operating policies of another undertaking with a view to gaining economic benefits from its activities.

DOMINANT INFLUENCE

Influence that can be exercised to achieve the operating and financial policies desired by the holder of influence.

EQUITY METHOD

A method of accounting for an investment that brings into the consolidated income statement the investor's share of the investment undertaking's results and that records in the balance sheet the investment undertaking's net assets including any goodwill arising (to the extent that it has not been previously written off).

Accounting

A parent undertaking should prepare consolidated financial statements for its group unless it uses one of the exemptions below:

a)   the group is small or medium-sized (as defined by the Companies Act)

b)   the subsidiary is merely held for resale

c)   the parent is itself a subsidiary

d)   severe long-term restrictions substantially hinder control

e)   there would be disproportionate expense and undue delay

f)   the subsidiary's activities are so different from the rest of the group's activities.

Note: that whilst reasons e) and f) exist under UK law and the IAS, the IAS really does not consider them valid reasons not to consolidate.

Accounting for investments in the parent company's accounts

In a parent's separate financial statements investments in subsidiaries should be:

a)   carried at cost;

b)   accounted for using the equity method; or

c)   accounted for as an available for sale financial asset as described in IAS 39 Financial Instruments.

Apart from the fact that they are the accounts of the company in which external shareholders invest, the accounts of the parent are really not normally of great significance. Carrying the investments in subsidiaries at historical cost is all that is needed. The consolidated accounts will reveal the latest carrying value of the component subsidiaries.

Disclosure

A list of all significant subsidiaries including their name, country of incorporation or residence, proportion of ownership interest, and if different, proportion of voting power held.

Minority interests should be presented in the consolidated balance sheet separately from liabilities and parent shareholders' equity. Minority interests in the income of the group should also be separately presented.

Problem areas and questions to ask about the accounts

WHAT HAS BEEN CONSOLIDATED?

Are all subsidiaries included? Consolidation is required not only where 50% or more of shares are owned by a parent but where there is effective control. UK law was specifically changed a few years ago, to ensure that entities controlled by a parent could not be left out of consolidation by having apparent control below the 50% level. One of the issues with Enron was about levels of ownership of entities* (the assets and particularly liabilities) that should be brought into Enron group accounts – the driving issue was to take liabilities/debt off the balance sheet.

* So called special purpose vehicles – see chapter 9.4.

CONSISTENT FIGURES

Has full disclosure been made for companies that have year end dates different from that of the parent?

Are accounting policies used throughout the group consistent or if not, have appropriate adjustments and disclosures been made in the consolidated accounts?

Have all inter-company transactions been properly eliminated?

Key differences

The requirement for the production of consolidated accounts is generally universal. The US authorities are looking at tightening up the issue of what constitutes a subsidiary.

Objective and definitions from the Standard

Objective

Note: this objective is from the UK FRS 2 as there is no objective in IAS 27.

The objective of this FRS is to require parent undertakings to provide financial information about the economic activities of their groups by preparing consolidated financial statements. These statements are intended to present financial information about a parent undertaking and its subsidiary undertakings as a single economic entity to show the economic resources controlled by the group, the obligations of the group and the results the group achieves with its resources.

Definitions

Control is the power to govern the financial and operating policies of an entity so as to obtain benefits from its activities.

A **subsidiary** is an entity including an unincorporated entity such as a partnership, that is controlled by another entity (known as the parent).

A **parent** is an entity that has one or more subsidiaries.

A **group** is a parent and all its subsidiaries.

Consolidated financial statements are the financial statements of a group presented as those of a single economic entity.

Minority interest is that portion of the profit or loss net assets of a subsidiary attributable to equity interests that are not owned, directly or indirectly through subsidiaries, by the parent.

The cost method is a method of accounting whereby the investment is recognised at cost. The investor recognises income from the investment only to the extent that the investor receives distributions from accumulated net profits of the investee arising after the date of acquisition.

6.3
Accounting for investments in associates – IAS 28

Why needed

A company can own 7%, 24%, 38% etc. of another company or enterprise. The question is, how should the net assets and results of these different levels of ownership be accounted for? Without some definition the owner could include or exclude, net assets (or liabilities) and shares of profits or losses as they saw fit.

Ideas – concepts

The issue to be addressed is how to account for substantial investments in other entities that are neither subsidiaries nor joint ventures. A simplistic but logical view would be if percentage ownership was considered. A range of 20%-50% ownership would indicate that the investing company has influence over the business in which it has invested – over the associate. With this range of ownership the investing business would be expected to have some rights with respect to the management, dividend payment and the use of assets of the associate. The underlying concept is that the share of worth or net assets, and results of this substantially owned (but not controlled or jointly managed) entity, should be brought into the investing businesses or group accounts. The alternative (required for ownership below the 20% threshold or where influence is restricted) is only to recognize dividends from the owned entity – a prudent approach.

ASSOCIATE VERSUS JOINT VENTURE

The difference between say a 33.33% holding in an associate and a similar percentage investment in a joint venture is that a joint venture has an agreement where the influence is joint and control is jointly agreed with other parties. In an associate the holding may give 'significant influence' but no joint control. In a joint venture each venturer has the power of veto over key decisions.

Key terms

An **associate** is an enterprise in which the investor has significant influence and which is neither a subsidiary nor a joint venture of the investor.

Significant influence is the power to participate in the financial and operating policy decisions of the investee, but is not control over those policies.

Accounting

Associates should be accounted for using the equity method unless there is restricted influence (in which case it is unlikely to be an associate and should be carried under the cost method – see IAS 27 Consolidated and Separate Financial Statements).

If an investment is acquired and held exclusively with a view to its subsequent disposal within twelve months from acquisition it shall be accounted for in accordance with IAS 39 Financial Instruments, at fair value with changes in fair value included in the profit or loss of the period of the change.

Disclosure

Investments in associates accounted for under the equity method should be disclosed as long-term fixed asset investments as a separate line on the balance sheet.

The investor's share of profits or losses of associates should be disclosed as a separate line on the income statement.

The fair value of investments in associates for which there are published price quotations should be disclosed.

There should be summarised financial information regarding the associates.

Problem areas and questions to ask about the accounts

IS THERE SIGNIFICANT INFLUENCE?

Significance influence can be evidenced in one or more of the following ways:

a) Representation on the board of directors or equivalent governing body.

b) Participation in the policy-making processes.

c) Material transactions between the investor and the associate.

d) Interchange or management personnel.

e) Provision of essential commercial and technical information.

IS THERE RESTRICTED INFLUENCE?

Ownership of less than 20% of the voting power is deemed to indicate no significant influence unless influence could be clearly demonstrated – by compliance with one or more of the indicators of significant influence above.

CONTINGENCIES

The investing business should disclose its share of any contingent liabilities of the associate and in particular contingent liabilities that arise if the investor business is severally liable for all the liabilities of the associate.

Key differences

Objective and definitions from the Standard

Note: this objective is from the UK FRS 9 as there is no objective in IAS 28.

Objective

The objective of this Standard is to reflect the effect on an investor's financial position and performance of its interests in associates for whose activities it is partly accountable because of the closeness of its involvement, as a result of its participating interest and significant influence.

Definitions

An **associate** is an entity, including an unincorporated entity such as a partnership, in which the investor has significant influence and which is neither a subsidiary nor a joint venture of the investor.

Significant influence is the power to participate in the financial and operating policy decisions of the investee but is not control or joint over those policies.

Control is the power to govern the financial and operating policies of an entity so as to obtain benefits from its activities.

Joint control is the contractually agreed sharing of control over an economic activity.

A **subsidiary** is an entity, including an unincorporated entity such as a partnership, that is controlled by another entity (known as the parent).

The **equity method** is a method of accounting whereby the investment is initially recorded at cost and adjusted thereafter for the post acquisition change in the investor's share of net assets of the investee. The profit or loss of the investor includes the investor's share of the profit or loss of the investee.

6.4

Financial reporting of interests in joint ventures – IAS 31

Why needed

Businesses frequently enter into agreements with other businesses to share resources, expertise etc. with a view to achieving jointly that which would be difficult or impossible to achieve on their own – they enter into joint ventures.

The joint venture activities may be undertaken and accounted for in different ways. The issues are what details of the jointly owned assets, liabilities, income and expenses should be disclosed.

The objective of this Standard is to reflect the effect on an investor's financial position and performance of its interests in a joint venture, for whose activities it is partly accountable, because of the closeness of its involvement, as a result of its long-term interest and joint control.

Ideas – concepts

Joint ventures are classified into three types:

1   jointly controlled
2   operations
3   assets and entities.

Jointly controlled operations and assets are really similar. It is for convenience that businesses share operations and assets jointly. Two or more businesses carry on their own business, the only link being the common use of assets or operations. Accounting for them is obvious and straightforward. The investor records its share of assets, liabilities, income and expenses in its own financial statements.

The jointly controlled entity operates as a business in its own right. A jointly controlled entity could be a partnership or some other legal structure; commonly limited companies are used. The recommended benchmark treatment is to proportionally consolidate the share of assets, liabilities, income and expenses of the joint venture business as at the balance sheet date. The rationale for this is that 'joint control' is just that. The investor has full rights of access and control over its proportion of net assets and income, and thus all relevant figures should be consolidated along with those of other group joint ventures and subsidiaries.

JOINT VENTURE VERSUS ASSOCIATE

The difference between say a 33.33% holding in a joint venture and an investment in an associate is that the joint venture holding has an agreement where the influence is joint and control is jointly agreed with other parties. In an associate the holding may give 'significant influence' but no joint control – the majority shareholder has power of veto.

Key terms

A **joint venture** is a contractual arrangement whereby two or more parties undertake an economic activity which is subject to joint control.

Proportionate consolidation means the inclusion of the venturer's share of assets and liabilities and income and expenditure.

Accounting

Joint ventures have to be classified as above.

Jointly controlled operations: a venturer should recognize its share of assets, liabilities, income and expenses.

Jointly controlled assets: a venturer should recognize its share of jointly controlled assets, appropriately classified, details of any liabilities – shared or jointly, any income from the sale or use of its share of the output and share of expenses.

Jointly controlled entities should be proportionately consolidated, combining items with the groups figures or identifying joint venture assets, liabilities, income and expenses separately. (Current UK practice is to show items separately on the face of the balance sheet and P&L account – the gross equity method.)

The equity method is an allowed (but not encouraged) alternative.

If a venturer has investments that are held under sever restrictions, or are held with a view to subsequent disposal, then they should be initially recognized at cost but subject to review for impairment (IAS 39).

Disclosure

The names of the joint venture businesses, partnerships, companies etc., there place of business and the shareholding should be disclosed.

If a venturer has guaranteed or has potential liabilities in respect of a joint venture, then the facts should be disclosed.

Problem areas and questions to ask about the accounts

CLASSIFICATION

Has the joint venture been correctly classified? Incorrect classification will lead to incorrect accounting.

TRANSACTIONS BETWEEN JV'S AND THE INVESTOR

It is possible that an investor could have arrangements such as sale of goods on 'a sale or return' basis with its joint venture entity. Questions could arise over the date of sale and thus when profit should be recognized. Adjustment should be made for only the group element of any unrealized profit.

It is the commercial reality or substance of any transactions that is to be recognized, not merely the legal form of any arrangement.

SPECIAL PURPOSE VEHICLES (SPV'S)

The use of spv's was at the heart of the Enron scandal! Special purpose vehicles could be any type of entity – partnership, company, joint venture. The shareholding arrangements could be genuinely complex. For example, for proper commercial confidentiality an activity could be owned not directly by an investor (a 100% subsidiary), but by an accumulation of shareholdings.

Again what is required is the true substance of the ownership to be revealed. That is, if an investor effectively controls another entity then all assets, liabilities, income and expenses should be consolidated.

Key differences

US practice is being aligned with the IAS, particularly with respect to spv's.

Objective and definitions from the Standard

Objective

Note: this objective is from the UK FRS 9 as there is no objective in IAS 27.

The objective of this Standard is to reflect the effect on an investor's financial position and performance of its interests in a joint venture, for whose activities it is partly accountable because of the closeness of its involvement, and as a result of its long-term interest and joint control.

Definitions

A **joint venture** is a contractual arrangement whereby two or more parties undertake an economic activity which is subject to joint control.

Control is the power to govern the financial and operating policies of an economic activity so as to obtain benefits from it.

Joint control is the contractually agreed sharing of control over an economic activity.

Significant influence is the power to participate in the financial and operating policy decisions of an economic activity but is not control or joint control over those policies.

A **venturer** is a party to a joint venture and has joint control over that joint venture.

An **investor** in a joint venture is a party to a joint venture and does not have joint control over that joint venture.

Proportionate consolidation is a method of accounting and reporting, whereby a venturer's share of each of the assets, liabilities, income and expenses of a jointly controlled entity is combined on a line-by-line basis with similar items in the venturer's financial statements, or reported as separate line items in the venturer's financial statements.

The **equity method** is a method of accounting and reporting, whereby an interest in a jointly controlled entity is initially recorded at cost and adjusted thereafter, for the post acquisition change in the venturer's share of net assets of the jointly controlled entity. The income statement reflects the venturer's share of the results of operations of the jointly controlled entity.

Gross equity method is a form of equity method under which the investor's share of the aggregate gross assets and liabilities underlying the net amount included for the investment is shown on the face of the balance sheet and, in the profit and loss account, the investor's share of the investee's turnover is noted.

Segment reporting – IAS 14

Why needed

Key uses of financial statements are:

- to identify performance – returns on investment and margins; and
- to know the amount and existence of assets and liabilities – where capital is employed in the business.

In accounts with diverse business activities and operating in different countries, summary figures present the overall picture and no detailed analysis is possible. A detailed breakdown of the figures is required.

Note: It does seem questionable that an Accounting Standard should be needed for such a topic. For a listed company (to which this Standard applies) it might be assumed that the markets and analysts' pressures would demand full disclosure. This may not be the case though, as UK, US and IAS have had Standards in place for some time. This may indicate that some companies are reluctant to voluntarily disclose information.

Ideas – concepts

Where financial statements are an amalgam of various activities in different locations, the overall results and net assets are disclosed when the financial statements are consolidated. However, performance of the various activities and of various locations may be impossible to ascertain.

The concept of this Standard is simple: to break down and present an analysis of the constituent business net assets and activities, either on both a product/service or geographical basis. The most relevant basis is called the primary basis of disclosure and the other the secondary. A matrix of disclosures under both analyses is required.

The Standard is only mandatory for stock market listed companies, although other (private) companies can follow it. If the Standard is adopted then it must be complied with in its entirety.

Key terms

BUSINESS SEGMENT OR CLASS OF BUSINESS

A business segment or class of business, is a distinguishable component of an entity that provides a separate product or service, or a separate group of related products or services.

GEOGRAPHICAL SEGMENT

A geographical segment is a geographical area comprising an individual country or group of countries, in which an entity operates, or to which it supplies products or services.

Accounting

Segment information should be prepared in conformity with the accounting policies adopted by the consolidated group.

Disclosure

Primary disclosure, the base being either business activities or geographical.

An enterprise should disclose for each reportable segment:

- external and internal revenue and results;
- the total carrying amount of segment assets and liabilities;
- cost of fixed assets acquired in the year;
- expense of depreciation and amortisation;
- significant non-cash flow expenses; and
- share of profit or losses of associates, joint ventures and investments.

Secondary disclosure, the base being that one NOT chosen as the primary! That is by geographical area or business activity revenue, total carrying amount of assets, cost of fixed assets acquired.

The idea is to give a matrix of information on both a business activity and geographical basis. The enterprise has to decide what the primary analysis base is to be, but the Standard does give guidance.

Problem areas and questions to ask about the accounts

DETAIL REQUIRED

The Standard is fairly demanding in the amount of detail required. However, it is very likely that multinationals will disclose this information and more, either because of good corporate governance or pressures of markets and analysts.

DIFFERENCES IN GAAP

There are no significant differences but:

- UK and IAS GAAP differ in how to identify geographical segments.

- The UK Standard has no primary/secondary distinction and requires less detail. US GAAP requires even more detail, e.g. R&D expenditure.

Objective and definitions from the Standard

Objective

The objective of this Standard is to establish principles for reporting financial information by segment – information about the different types of products and services an enterprise produces, and different geographical areas in which it operates – to help users of financial statements:

a) better understand the enterprise's past performance;

b) better assess the enterprise's risks and returns; and

c) make more informed judgements about the enterprise as a whole.

Definitions

A **business segment** is a distinguishable component of an enterprise that is engaged in providing an individual product or service, or a group of related products or services and that is subject to risks and returns that are different from those of other business segments. Factors that should be considered in determining whether products and services are related include:

a) the nature of the products or services;

b) the nature of the production processes;

c) the type or class of customer for the products or services;

d) the methods used to distribute the products or provide the services; and

e) if applicable, the nature of the regulatory environment, for example, banking insurance, or public utilities.

A **geographical segment** is a distinguishable component of an enterprise that is engaged in providing products or services within a particular economic environment, and that is subject to risks and returns that are different from those of components operating in other economic environments. Factors that should be considered include:

a) similarity of economic and political conditions;

b) relationships between operations in different geographical areas;

c) proximity of operations;

d) special risks associated with operations in a particular area;

e) exchange control regulations; and

f) the underlying currency risks.

A **reportable segment** is a business segment or a geographical segment identified based on the foregoing definitions for which the segment information is required to be disclosed by this Standard.

Accounting policies are the specific principles, bases, conventions, rules and practices adopted by an enterprise in preparing and presenting financial statements.

Revenue is the gross inflow of economic benefits during the period arising in the course of the ordinary activities of an enterprise, when those inflows result in increases in equity, other than increases relating to contributions from equity participants.

Operating activities are the principal revenue producing activities of the enterprise and other activities that are not investing or financing activities.

Segment revenue is revenue reported in the enterprise's income statement that is directly attributable to a segment, and the relevant portion of enterprise revenue that can be allocated on a reasonable basis to a segment.

Segment expense is expense resulting from the operating activities of a segment that is directly attributable to the segment and the relevant portion of an expense that can be allocated on a reasonable basis to the segment.

Segment result is segment revenue, less segment expense.

Segment assets are those operating assets that are employed by a segment in its operating activities and that are either directly attributable to the segment, or can be allocated to the segment on a reasonable basis.

Segment liabilities are those operating liabilities that result from the operating activities of a segment in its operating activities, and that are either directly attributable to the segment, or can be allocated to the segment on a reasonable basis.

SEVEN

Specialized industries

7.1

Accounting and reporting by retirement benefit plans – IAS 26

Why needed

Investors, but maybe more so employees (prospective pensioners), and existing pensioners need to know whether a business's pension scheme is adequately funded. Retirement benefit plans or pension schemes are for the benefit of employees past and present. The accounts of such funds should clearly and fairly state the basis on which assets and liabilities are recognised and valued in the scheme's balance sheet.

Ideas – concepts

Balance sheets of investment funds – for retirement benefits or pensions, could be drawn up on many different bases. What is needed is an up to date value of the investment assets along with a calculation of future liabilities (expressed in today's terms). If these are in balance the scheme is adequately funded. If the present value of future liabilities is in excess of the fair value of the schemes assets then the scheme is under funded.

Key terms

Pension schemes or retirement benefit plans are arrangements whereby an enterprise provides benefits for its employees on retirement.

Defined contribution plans are retirement benefit plans under which set amounts are paid into funds to provide for retirement benefits – there are no commitments or guarantees as to what the benefits on retirement will be.

Defined benefit plans are retirement benefit plans under which amounts to be paid as retirement benefits are determined by reference to a formula, usually based on employee's earnings and/or years of service.

Funding is the transfer of assets to a fund separate from the employer's enterprise to meet future obligations for the payment of retirement benefits.

Actuarial present value of promised retirement benefits is the present value of the expected payments by a retirement benefit plan to existing and past employees, attributable to the service already rendered.

Accounting

VALUATION OF SCHEME OR PLAN ASSETS

Retirement benefit plan investments should be carried at fair value.

Disclosure

FOR DEFINED CONTRIBUTION PLANS

A report should disclose the following:

a) a statement of net assets available for benefits, changes in net assets available for benefits and a description of the funding policy;

b) a summary of significant accounting policies; and

c) a description of the plan and any changes in the plan during the period.

FOR DEFINED BENEFIT PLANS

A report should disclose a statement of net assets available for benefits and the actuarial present value of promised retirement benefits (distinguishing between vested and non-vested benefits*), and thus the resulting surplus or deficit of the plan's fund.

* Vested benefits are those that the business is absolutely committed to pay – their payment does not depend on continuing employment of the employee.

An alternative is allowed: that the actuarial present value of the promised retirement benefits be shown as a note rather than in a statement that arrives at a surplus or deficit figure.

Any changes in actuarial assumptions should be disclosed.

The actuarial valuation should be at the date of the report but if earlier, the valuation date should be disclosed.

Problem areas and questions to ask about the accounts

INDEPENDENCE OF TRUSTEES

This is not really an accounting issue. The trustees of a business's pension fund should ensure that they are independent (e.g. they are not all directors or shareholders of the business). The UK and most countries will have legislation that ensures this is the case.

Objective and definitions from the Standard

Objective

Note: there is no objective in IAS 26.

Definitions

Retirement benefit plans are arrangements whereby an enterprise provides benefits for its employees on or after termination of service (either in the form of an annual income or a lump sum), when such benefits, or the employer's contributions towards them, can be determined or estimated in advance of retirement from the provisions of a document, or from the enterprise's practices.

Defined contribution plans are retirement benefit plans under which amounts to be paid as retirement benefits are determined by contributions to a fund, together with investment earnings thereon.

Defined benefit plans are retirement benefit plans under which amounts to be paid as retirement benefits are determined by reference to a formula usually based on employee's earnings and/or years of service.

Funding is the transfer of assets to an entity (the fund) separate from the employer's enterprise, to meet future obligations for the payment of retirement benefits.

Participants are the members of the retirement benefit plan and others who are entitled to benefits under the plan.

Net assets available for benefits are the assets of a plan, less liabilities other than the actuarial present value of promised retirement plan benefits.

Actuarial present value of promised retirement benefits is the present value of the expected payments by a retirement benefit plan to existing and past employees, attributable to the service already rendered.

Vested benefits are benefits, the rights of which, under the conditions of a retirement benefit plan, are not conditional on continued employment.

Disclosures in the financial statements of banks and similar financial institutions – IAS 30

Why needed

Banks are special businesses. They are vital in most economies, as without them it would be very difficult to trade and economic activity would be very much slower.

Successful banking depends on managing lending to customers, short and long-term, this being financed partially by the banks shareholders' equity but mostly by deposits from investors. If the amounts lent and managed, and their maturity dates get out of balance then the bank could have severe, if not fatal liquidity problems. There are internationally agreed levels of shareholders' equity and profiles of loans – the Basle Convention rules. These rules aim to ensure the safe operation of banks. Since economies and banks are so closely inter-related the Basle Convention is also a vital support for the soundness of economies worldwide.

To enable regulators, investors and customers to confirm that banks are sound financially requires proper disclosure in amount and particularly classification of liabilities and assets – this Standard aims to ensure proper disclosure of the necessary information.

Ideas – concepts

The fundamental concepts for banks reporting must be to ensure that assets and liabilities and their maturity dates are disclosed. For those involved with the bank to be sure that the bank can fund loans and repay obligations when due – that there are sufficient funds available at the right time.

There should be no netting off – gross assets and liabilities should be disclosed.

The maturity of investments (deposits held by the bank) and loans granted should be disclosed.

Another concept is that risk assessment and exposure should be disclosed. Whilst encouraged in this Standard, IAS 32 and IAS 32 on Financial Instruments make much more detailed demands for accountability and disclosure.

Key terms

Note: there are no definitions in IAS 30.

Liquidity is having adequate, immediately available short-term funds to meet immediate and short-term liabilities.

Tier Capital are amounts of shareholders' funds and other capital available as a base for banking operations. Capital is defined in different tiers; these relate to whether the capital is the shareholders' equity or funds the bank has borrowed. The amounts and repayment dates of the capital is a vital issue.

Hedging for accounting purposes, means designating one or more hedging instrument (a derivative, financial asset or liability) so that their change in fair value is an offset, in whole or part, to the change in fair value or cash flows of a hedged item.

Fair value is the amount for which an asset could be exchanged or a liability settled between knowledgeable willing parties in an arm's length transaction.

Accounting

Specific accounting policies should be disclosed. Where appropriate policies in respect of:

a) principal types of income;

b) the valuation of investment and dealing securities;

c) the distinction between balance sheet assets and liabilities and contingent assets and liabilities;

d) the basis of determination of loan write offs; or

e) the basis of determination of charges for general banking.

Disclosure

INCOME STATEMENT

A bank should disclose the principal amounts of income and expenses under appropriate headings. Income and expenses should not be offset except for those relating to hedges or where the related assets/liabilities are permitted to be offset.

Appropriate headings will include:

- interest income and expense
- dividend income
- fee and commission income and expense
- gains less losses arising from investing and dealing activities
- losses on loans and advances
- general administrative expense
- other income and expenses.

BALANCE SHEET

A bank should present a balance sheet that groups assets and liabilities by nature and lists them in an order that reflects their relative liquidity. The amount at which an asset or liability is stated in the balance sheet should not be offset by the deduction of another liability or asset, unless a legal right of set-off exists.

A bank should disclose the fair values of each class of its financial assets and liabilities, as required by IAS 32 and IAS 39 on financial Instruments.

Appropriate headings will include:

ASSETS

- cash and balances with central banks
- government and other securities held for dealing purposes
- loans and advances to other banks or in the money market
- loans and advances to customers
- investment securities

LIABILITIES

- deposits from other banks or the money markets
- amounts owed to other depositors
- certificates, promissory notes and other liabilities evidence by paper
- other borrowed funds

The above assets and liabilities should be analysed into relevant maturity groupings.

Any major concentration, in a particular area, with a particular customer or industry, of assets and liabilities (on or off balance sheet) should be disclosed.

Disclosure should be made of any security linked to assets and liabilities.

CONTINGENCIES AND COMMITMENTS

A bank should classify and disclose contingent liabilities and commitments.

LOSSES ON LOANS

A bank should disclose the accounting policy which describes the basis on which loans are recognised as an expense – their bad debt policy.

Disclosure of movements on bad debt provisions and where loans are neither being repaid nor interest is being received, should also be made.

Problem areas and questions to ask about the accounts

COMPLIANCE WITH BANKING RULES

Compliance with national or international banking rules may require more disclosure than this basic Standard requires.

COMPLIANCE WITH IAS 32 AND IAS 39 – FINANCIAL INSTRUMENTS

Since the majority of a bank's transactions involve dealing in financial instruments then the above Standards must be referred to.

Objective and definitions from the Standard

Objective

Note: these words are taken from the Scope of the Standard as there is no objective in IAS 30.

Banks represent a significant and influential sector of business worldwide. Banks play a major role in maintaining confidence in the monetary system through their close relationship with regulatory authorities and governments, and the regulations imposed on them by those governments. The operations and thus accounting and reporting requirements of banks are different from those of other commercial enterprises. This Standard recognizes banks, special needs. It also encourages the presentation of a commentary on the financial statements which deals with such matters as the management and control of liquidity and risk.

Definitions

Note: there are no additional definitions in IAS 30.

Agriculture – IAS 41

Why needed

Agriculture is obviously a specialized area of business and thus accounting is specialized. Maybe this should be one of many Standards that cover specific industries.

Ideas – concepts

What is the value of herds of beasts or crops? Many different values could be used. Unless growth is complete some crops are worthless, other crops or animals increase in value until they are ripe for harvesting or are fully mature.

To avoid selection of the most favourable (high or maybe low valuation) the Standard demands consistency in that agricultural produce is valued at fair value.

Key terms

Agricultural produce is the harvested product of the enterprise's biological assets.

Accounting

A biological asset should be measured on initial recognition and thereafter at its fair value.

Disclosure

Appropriate accounting policies that comply with the Standard should be disclosed.

Problem areas and questions to ask about the accounts

KNOWLEDGE OF THE INDUSTRY

Agricultural and farming businesses are highly specialized and crop and herd values, including net realizable values, need to be properly determined.

The industry is also subject to wide support through subsidies and grants. The economic and political pressures on the industry need to be understood.

DIFFERENCES IN GAAP

There is no corresponding UK Standard.

Objective and definitions from the Standard

Objective

The objective of this Standard is to prescribe the accounting treatment, financial statement presentation and disclosures related to agricultural activity.

Definitions

Agricultural activity is the management by an enterprise of the biological transformation of biological assets for sale, into agricultural produce, or into biological assets.

Agricultural produce is the harvested product of the enterprise's biological assets.

A **biological asset** is a living animal or plant.

Biological transformation comprises the process of growth, degeneration, production, and procreation that cause qualitative or quantitative change in a biological asset.

A **group of biological assets** is an aggregation of similar living animals or plants.

Harvest is the detachment of produce from a biological asset at the cessation of a biological asset's life processes.

An **active market** where all of the conditions exist:

a) the items traded within the market are homogeneous;

b) willing buyers and sellers can normally be found at any time; and

c) prices are available to the public.

Fair value is the amount for which an asset could be exchanged between knowledgeable, willing parties in an arm's length transaction.

Carrying amount is the amount at which an asset is recognized in the balance sheet.

Government grants are as defined in IAS 20 Accounting for Government Grants and Disclosure of Government Assistance.

7.4

Insurance contracts – IFRS 4

Why needed

Accounting practices for insurance contracts have been diverse, and have often differed from practices in other sectors. This standard is a first phase aimed at improving accounting for insurance and requiring disclosure of information about such contracts. The adoption of IFRS by many entities and increased scrutiny and regulation of the insurance sector are other drivers for IFRS's for this specialised sector.

The IFRS applies to all insurance contracts (including reinsurance contracts) that an entity issues and to reinsurance contracts that it holds, except for specified contracts covered by other IFRSs. It does not apply to other assets and liabilities of an insurer, such as financial assets and financial liabilities within the scope of IAS 39 Financial Instruments: Recognition and Measurement. Nor does it address accounting by policyholders.

Ideas – concepts

Insurance contracts are not like buying and selling goods in a supermarket. There the transaction (the contract) is usually concluded in a very short timescale with definite amounts of income, costs and profit. Insurance contracts can extend over years, the extent of liability (cost) may be virtually nil or large. The crystallisation of the liability (and cost) will depend on future events which may or may not happen. Further, as there is an extended life to an insurance contract, sums need to be invested to cover future liabilities – the return on the investments (assets) will also depend on future events – prevailing interest rates, market conditions etc.

Thus there is much subjectivity behind many of the income, expense, asset and liability figures in the financial statements. There are many possible methods of accounting for assets/liabilities and profits/losses. There may be logic in netting off figures – eg were an insured amount is also reinsured by another entity.

The approach of this initial standard covering the insurance contracts is to align accounting with that set out in the IFRS framework, prohibit what is unacceptable practice and move accounting policies and disclosure towards what is considered best practice.

It is accepted that apart from treatment and disclosure which positively goes against the Framework and IAS 8 Accounting Policies, Changes in Accounting estimates and Errors, existing accounting policies may continue.

The three principal aims of the standards are to:

- Improve accounting policies and ensure they align with the Framework

- Carry out liability adequacy tests and if there is a shortfall the entire amount should be recognized as a charge in profit and loss.

- Require disclosure about the amount, timing and uncertainty of future cash flows.

Key terms

There is a comprehensive listing (given at the end of this chapter) of specific terms used both in the insurance industry and in this standard. The key terms are:

- **Insurance contract** is a contract under which one party (the insurer) accepts significant insurance risk from another party (the policyholder) by agreeing to compensate the policyholder if a specified uncertain future event (the insured event) adversely affects the policyholder. (See Appendix B for guidance on this

- **Liability adequacy test** is an assessment of whether the carrying amount of an insurance liability needs to be increased (or the carrying amount of related deferred acquisition costs or related intangible assets decreased), based on a review of future cash flows.

- **Insurance risk** is the risk, other than financial risk, transferred from the holder of a contract to the issuer. The aim is to make it clear that there are different risks ie risks of offering insurance are different from financial risks – risks associated with market conditions, interest rates etc.

Accounting – Recognition and measurement

TEMPORARY EXEMPTION FROM SOME OTHER IFRSS

Paragraphs 10-12 of IAS 8 *Accounting Policies, Changes in Accounting Estimates and Errors* specify criteria for an entity to use in developing an accounting policy if no IFRS applies specifically to an item. However, this IFRS exempts an insurer from applying those criteria to its accounting policies for:

a) insurance contracts that it issues (including related acquisition costs and related intangible assets, such as those described in paragraphs 31 and 32 of the standard); and

b) reinsurance contracts that it holds.

However the IFRS does not exempt an insurer from some implications of the criteria in paragraphs 10-12 of IAS 8.

Specifically, an insurer:

a) shall not recognise as a liability any provisions for possible future claims, if those claims arise under insurance contracts that are not in existence at the reporting date (such as catastrophe provisions and equalisation provisions).

b) shall carry out the liability adequacy test as below.

c) shall remove an insurance liability (or a part of an insurance liability) from its balance sheet when, and only when, it is extinguished-ie when the obligation specified in the contract is discharged or cancelled or expires.

d) shall not offset (net off):

   i) *reinsurance assets* against the related insurance liabilities; or

   ii) income or expense from reinsurance contracts against the expense or income from the related insurance contracts.

e) shall consider whether its reinsurance assets are impaired

LIABILITY ADEQUACY TEST

An insurer shall assess at each reporting date whether its recognised insurance liabilities are adequate, using current estimates of future cash flows under its insurance contracts. If that assessment shows that the carrying amount of its insurance liabilities (less related deferred acquisition costs and related intangible assets) is inadequate in the light of the estimated future cash flows, the entire deficiency shall be recognised in profit or loss. If an insurer applies a liability adequacy test that meets specified minimum requirements, this IFRS imposes no further requirements.

IMPAIRMENT OF REINSURANCE ASSETS

If a cedant's reinsurance asset is impaired, the cedant shall reduce its carrying amount accordingly and recognise that impairment loss in profit or loss. A reinsurance asset is impaired if, and only if:

a) there is objective evidence, as a result of an event that occurred after initial recognition of the reinsurance asset, that the cedant may not receive all amounts due to it under the terms of the contract; and

b) that event has a reliably measurable impact on the amounts that the cedant will receive from the reinsurer.

CHANGES IN ACCOUNTING POLICIES

An insurer may change its accounting policies for insurance contracts if, and only if, the change makes the financial statements more relevant to the economic decision-making needs of users and no less reliable, or more reliable and no less relevant to those needs. An insurer shall judge relevance and reliability by the criteria in IAS 8.

Prudence An insurer need not change its accounting policies for insurance contracts to eliminate excessive prudence. However, if an insurer already measures its insurance contracts with sufficient prudence, it shall not introduce additional prudence.

If relevant the following specific issues should be considered.

- **Current market interest**
- **Continuation of existing practices**
- **Future investment margins**
- **Shadow accounting.**
- **Insurance contracts acquired in a business combination or portfolio transfer**
- **Discretionary participation features**
- **Discretionary participation features in financial instruments**

Disclosure

An insurer shall disclose information that identifies and explains the amounts in its financial statements arising from insurance contracts. To comply an insurer shall disclose:

a) its accounting policies for insurance contracts and related assets, liabilities, income and expense.

b) the recognised assets, liabilities, income and expense (and, if it presents its cash flow statement using the direct method, cash flows) arising from insurance contracts. Furthermore, if the insurer is a cedant, it shall disclose:

   i) gains and losses recognised in profit or loss on buying reinsurance; and

   ii) if the cedant defers and amortises gains and losses arising on buying reinsurance, the amortisation for the period and the amounts remaining unamortised at the beginning and end of the period.

c) the process used to determine the assumptions that have the greatest effect on the measurement of the recognised amounts described in (b). When practicable, an insurer shall also give quantified disclosure of those assumptions.

d) the effect of changes in assumptions used to measure insurance assets and insurance liabilities, showing separately the effect of each change that has a material effect on the financial statements.

e) reconciliations of changes in insurance liabilities, reinsurance assets and, if any, related deferred acquisition costs.

AMOUNT, TIMING AND UNCERTAINTY OF CASH FLOWS

An insurer shall disclose information that helps users to understand the amount, timing and uncertainty of future cash flows from insurance contracts.

An insurer shall disclose:

a) its objectives in managing risks arising from insurance contracts and its policies for mitigating those risks.

b) those terms and conditions of insurance contracts that have a material effect on the amount, timing and uncertainty of the insurer's future cash flows.

c) information about insurance risk (both before and after risk mitigation by reinsurance), including information about:

  i) the sensitivity of profit or loss and equity to changes in variables that have a material effect on them.

  ii) concentrations of insurance risk.

  iii) actual claims compared with previous estimates (ie claims development). The disclosure about claims development shall go back to the period when the earliest material claim arose for which there is still uncertainty about the amount and timing of the claims payments, but need not go back more than ten years. An insurer need not disclose this information for claims for which uncertainty about the amount and timing of claims payments is typically resolved within one year.

d) the information about interest rate risk and credit risk that IAS 32 would require if the insurance contracts were within the scope of IAS 32.

e) information about exposures to interest rate risk or market risk under embedded derivatives contained in a host insurance contract if the insurer is not required to, and does not, measure the embedded derivatives at fair value.

REDESIGNATION OF FINANCIAL ASSETS

When an insurer changes its accounting policies for insurance liabilities, it is permitted, but not required, to reclassify some or all of its financial assets as 'at fair value through profit or loss'. This reclassification is permitted if an insurer changes accounting policies when it first applies this IFRS and if it makes a subsequent policy change permitted by this IFRS. The reclassification is a change in accounting policy and IAS 8 applies.

Problems areas and questions to ask about the accounts

Embedded derivatives IAS 39 requires an entity to separate some embedded derivatives from their host contract, measure them at *fair value*. There may be embedded derivatives in insurance contracts.

Unbundling of deposit components Some insurance contracts contain both an insurance component and a deposit component.

AMENDMENTS TO OTHER IFRSS

IAS 18 *Revenue* is amended to require the correct recognition of income streams that can arise from insurance contracts – *Origination fees and Investment management fees*. The revision to IAS18 defines what is meant by these terms and how the income is to be accounted for.

IAS 19 Employee Benefits – a qualifying insurance policy is re defined.

In IAS 37 Provisions, Contingent Liabilities and Contingent Assets clarification is given as to how the Standard applies to provisions, contingent liabilities and contingent assets of an insurer, other than those arising from its contractual obligations and rights under insurance contracts within the scope of IFRS 4.

IAS 40 Investment properties. Entities may operate internal property funds – guidance is given s to how these properties should be valued and accounted for.

Objective and definitions from the standard

Objective

The objective of this IFRS is to specify the financial reporting for insurance contracts by any entity that issues such contracts (described in this IFRS as an insurer) until the Board completes the second phase of its project on insurance contracts. In particular, this IFRS requires:

a) limited improvements to accounting by insurers for insurance contracts.

b) disclosure that identifies and explains the amounts in an insurer's financial statements arising from insurance contracts and helps users of those financial statements understand the amount, timing and uncertainty of future cash flows from insurance contracts.

Definitions

Cedant is the policyholder under a reinsurance contract.

Deposit component is a contractual component that is not accounted for as a derivative under IAS 39 and would be within the scope of IAS 39 if it were a separate instrument.

Direct insurance contract is an insurance contract that is not a reinsurance contract.

Discretionary participation feature is a contractual right to receive, as a supplement to guaranteed benefits, additional benefits:

a) that are likely to be a significant portion of the total contractual benefits;

b) whose amount or timing is contractually at the discretion of the issuer; and

c) that are contractually based on:

   i)   the performance of a specified pool of contracts or a specified type of contract;

   ii) realised and/or unrealised investment returns on a specified pool of assets held by the issuer; or

   iii) the profit or loss of the company, fund or other entity that issues the contract.

Fair value is the amount for which an asset could be exchanged, or a liability settled, between knowledgeable, willing parties in an arm's length transaction.

Financial risk is the risk of a possible future change in one or more of a specified interest rate, financial instrument price, commodity price, foreign exchange rate, index of prices or rates, credit rating or credit index or other variable, provided in the case of a non-financial variable that the variable is not specific to a party to the contract.

Guaranteed benefits are payments or other benefits to which a particular policyholder or investor has an unconditional right that is not subject to the contractual discretion of the issuer.

A guaranteed element is an obligation to pay guaranteed benefits, included in a contract that contains a discretionary participation feature.

Insurance asset is an insurer's net contractual rights under an insurance contract.

Insurance contract is a contract under which one party (the insurer) accepts significant insurance risk from another party (the policyholder) by agreeing to compensate the policyholder if a specified uncertain future event (the insured event) adversely affects the policyholder. (See Appendix B for guidance on this definition.)

Insurance liability is an insurer's net contractual obligations under an insurance contract.

Insurance risk is the risk, other than financial risk, transferred from the holder of a contract to the issuer.

Insured event is an uncertain future event that is covered by an insurance contract and creates insurance risk.

Insurer is the party that has an obligation under an insurance contract to compensate a policyholder if an insured event occurs.

Liability adequacy test is an assessment of whether the carrying amount of an insurance liability needs to be increased (or the carrying amount of related deferred acquisition costs or related intangible assets decreased), based on a review of future cash flows.

Policyholder is the party that has a right to compensation under an insurance contract if an insured event occurs.

Reinsurance assets are a cedant's net contractual rights under a reinsurance contract.

Reinsurance contract is an insurance contract issued by one insurer (the reinsurer) to compensate another insurer (the cedant) for losses on one or more contracts issued by the cedant.

Reinsurer is the party that has an obligation under a reinsurance contract to compensate a cedant if an insured event occurs.

Unbundled is to account for the components of a contract as if they were separate contracts.

7.5

Exploration for and evaluation of mineral resources – IFRS 6

Why needed

There are differing views as to how exploration and evaluation expenditures should be accounted for and the topic is excluded from IAS 16 Property, plant and equipment and IAS 38 Intangible assets. There are inconsistencies with analogous items, eg accounting for research and development costs covered by IAS 38. Other extant accounting standards have diverse approaches. Thus there is need for a single acceptable approach, consistent with the IFRS framework and other existing IFRS's, especially for entities adopting IFRS

Ideas – concepts

The basic issue is whether the often sizeable initial expenses for evaluating and exploring for mineral resources should be written off as incurred (being prudent), or capitalised as an asset which is then depreciated or amortised over the life of the project (accruals concept).

The obvious 'safe bet' would be to require all costs to be written off as incurred until such times as a viable extraction and cash generating project was initiated. However exploration and evaluation expenses can be large amounts and not matching the costs to the future revenue streams would seriously distort the financial reporting of entities undertaking large and continuing exploration and evaluation projects.

The standard gives general guidance, permitting capitalisation of expenses associated with exploring and evaluating mineral resources. It permits existing accounting policies to be continued but does point to possibly improved disclosure. It specifically requires that any expenses capitalised as assets should be subject to impairment reviews and gives outline examples of signs of impairment.

Key terms

Exploration and evaluation expense is expense incurred in connection with exploration for and evaluation of mineral resources before the technical feasibility and commercial viability of the project for extracting mineral resources is proven.

Exploration and evaluation assets are exploration and evaluation expenditures which are capitalized and recognised as assets in an entities balance sheet.

Accounting

TEMPORARY EXEMPTION FROM SOME OTHER IFRSS

Paragraphs 11 and 12 of IAS 8 *Accounting Policies, Changes in Accounting Estimates and Errors* specify criteria for an entity to consider when developing accounting policies if no IFRS applies specifically to an item. This IFRS exempts an entity from applying the rigor of those criteria to its accounting policies for the recognition and measurement of exploration and evaluation assets.

BUT this standard does require a policy specifying which expenditures are recognized as exploration and evaluation assets and prohibits development costs being recognised as exploration and evaluation assets.

CHANGES IN ACCOUNTING POLICIES

An entity may change its accounting policies for exploration and evaluation expenditures if the change makes the financial statements more relevant to the economic decision making needs of users.

MEASUREMENT

At recognition exploration and evaluation assets shall be measured at cost.

The standard gives brief examples of what might constitute cost. The principal is that expenditure should be associated with finding specific mineral resources.

After recognition exploration and evaluation assets can be measure using the cost model or the revaluation model (as in IAS 16 Property plant and equipment, or IAS 38 Intangible assets)

IMPAIRMENT

Exploration and evaluation assets shall be assessed for impairment when facts and circumstances suggest that the carrying amount of an exploration and evaluation asset may exceed its recoverable amount. An entity shall measure, present and disclose any resulting impairment loss in accordance with IAS16, except that paragraph 20 of IFRS6 outlines facts that indicate the likely impairment of an exploration and evaluation asset.

LEVEL AT WHICH IMPAIRMENT IS TO BE TESTED

An entity shall determine an accounting policy for allocating exploration and evaluation assets to cash-generating units (or groups of units)for the purposes of assessing such assets for impairment. Units (or groups) should not be larger than a segment (primary or secondary reporting) as defined in IAS 14 Segment reporting.

Disclosure

PRESENTATION

An entity shall classify exploration and evaluation assets as tangible or intangible according to the nature of the assets acquired and apply the classification consistently.

An exploration and evaluation asset shall no longer be classified as such when technical feasibility and commercial viability of extracting a mineral resource is demonstrable. Before reclassification an exploration or evaluation asset should be tested for impairment and any impairment loss recognised.

ADDITIONAL INFORMATION

An entity shall disclose information that identifies and explains the amounts recognised in its financial statements arising from the exploration for an evaluation of mineral resources.

Problems areas and questions to ask about the accounts

WHAT EXPENDITURE CAN BE CAPITALISED?

The standard does give outline guidance and expenses must relate to a project for the likely successful extraction of mineral resources. However there can still be a range of what companies might consider as prudent to capitalise or write off. There needs to be a clear, consistently applied, policy.

Objective and definitions from the standard

Objective

The objective of this IFRS is to specify the financial reporting for the exploration for and evaluation of mineral resources.

In particular, the IFRS requires:

- limited improvements to existing accounting practices for exploration and evaluation expenditures.

- entities that recognize exploration and evaluation assets to assess such assets for impairment in accordance with this IFRS and measure any impairment in accordance with IAS 36 Impairment of Assets.

- disclosures that identify and explain the amounts in the entity's financial statements arising from the exploration for and evaluation of mineral resources and help users of those financial statements understand the amount, timing and certainty of future cash flows from any exploration and evaluation assets recognized.

Definitions

Exploration and evaluation assets are exploration and evaluation expenditures recognized as assets in accordance with the entity's accounting policy.

Exploration and evaluation expenditures are expenditures incurred by an entity in connection with exploration for and evaluation of mineral resources before the technical feasibility and commercial viability of extracting a mineral resource are demonstrable.

Exploration for and Evaluation of Mineral Resources is the search for mineral resources, including minerals, natural gas and similar non-regenerative resources after the entity has obtained the legal rights to explore in a specific area, as well as the determination of the technical feasibility and commercial viability of extracting the mineral resource.

EIGHT
Other

8.1
Financial reporting in hyperinflationary economies – IAS 29

Why needed

Some economies can be subject to periods of hyper-inflation. The problem is how to meaningfully report business results.

Ideas – concepts

If prices have increased by a factor of say 100 times over a year then historic figures for balance sheet items such as plant and equipment, inventories will give a totally unrealistic picture of the economic value to the business of the assets. Also, reported net profit or loss based on historic costs will be totally distorted.

The figures for the period in question should be adjusted as at the year end balance sheet date, either by adjusting the historic cost figures with indices that adjust to the measuring unit (or currency), or by adjusting relevant balance sheet and earnings statement figures to current cost.

Key terms

A **measuring unit** is an adjusted unit (of currency) used to report and measure financial performance. Adjustment is effected by using a general price index.

A **general price index** is a factor or indice that reflects the change in general purchasing power over a period.

Accounting

The financial statements of an enterprise that reports in the currency of a hyper-inflationary economy, whether they are based on a historical cost approach or a current cost approach, should be stated in terms of the measuring unit current at the balance sheet date.

The corresponding figures for the previous period and any information in respect of earlier periods should be stated in terms of the measuring unit current at the balance sheet date.

The gain or loss on the net monetary position should be included in net income and separately disclosed.

Disclosure

The following disclosures should be made:

a) the fact that the financial statements have been restated for the changes in the general purchasing power of the reporting currency and, as a result, are stated in terms of the measuring unit current at the balance sheet date;

b) whether the financial statements are based on a historical cost approach or a current cost approach; and

c) the identity and level of the price index at the balance sheet date and the movement in the index during the current and the previous reporting period.

Problem areas and questions to ask about the accounts

MAKING SENSE OF THE FIGURES

Whilst the Standard attempts to make reporting in times of hyper-inflation possible. The economic, social, political and other distortions to normal business operation may render any reporting of little value.

SELECTING A GENERAL PRICE INDEX

A truly general price index may be available and be the most appropriate for making adjustments. There may be more than one price change indice in which case, care should be taken in selection of what is meant to be a consistently based indice.

Objective and definitions from the Standard

This Standard is very much a statement of general principals on how to account for and disclose what is hopefully an uncommon problem. There is neither objective to the Standard nor a set of definitions.

NINE
Basic financial statements and other issues

9.1
Financial statement components and other issues

A set of financial statements (or accounts) should contain the following:

- A balance sheet
- A profit and loss account (P&L Account) or income statement
- Accounting policies and explanatory notes
- A cash flow statement
- A statement showing changes in equity

This section reviews:

- balance sheets and profit and loss accounts, showing what they are made up of and what they intend to convey;
- the accounting framework, concepts and conventions; and
- examples of cash flow statements – these are also covered in IAS 7 – Cash Flow Statements.

The balance sheet

A balance sheet is a statement showing net assets owned on one side and who owns and finances them on the other side, at a point in time.

Net Assets

Land, buildings, stocks, debtors less current liabilities (overdrafts, creditors)

=

Financed by

Shareholders funds (share capital and retained profits) and loans

What (in monetary terms) net assets or capital employed is used by the business and who finances that capital employed?

As far as possible it is desirable that period end balances show the up to date value to the business of the assets and the full extent of ownership and funding. BUT a balance sheet is not a valuation statement.

A VERY SIMPLE EXAMPLE:

Balance sheet at DATE period or year end

Assets employed in the business

Land and buildings		74
Motor vehicles		20
		94
Stocks	21	
Debtors	32	
Creditors	(18)	
		35
Total capital employed in the business		129 = X

Funding of the business

Long term loans		40
Shareholders' funds or equity		
Share capital	20	
Retained profits	69	
		89
Total funding or capital invested		129 = X

The profit and loss account or income statement

A profit and loss (P&L) account or income statement shows the sales, less costs/expenses for a period resulting in a profit or loss for the period.

A VERY SIMPLE EXAMPLE:

Profit and loss account for the period ended _____	
Sales	155
Costs and expenses	(137)
Profit for the period	18

These two principal financial statements are meant to show correctly and fairly where a business is at the end of the period (the balance sheet), and whether it has made a profit or loss for the period (the P&L account).

Different statement layouts

A major problem for users of financial statements is the existence of different layouts. This just has to be accepted. Though some harmonization has taken place, there is a long way to go till we get the definitive world-wide layout.

It is unlikely that Accounting Standards can bring complete harmony to balance sheet layouts and readers of financial statements have to cope with the different layouts – they can easily be rearranged to a familiar format. Published P&L or income statement layouts are likely to converge in that a new statement is envisaged.

Balance sheet layouts can be quite different in layout, but the content is the same. Set out below are 3 examples of balance sheet layouts, all using the same figures.

The first one is laid out for management purposes – clearly showing capital employed in the business on one side and capital invested on the other. This layout is essential if ratios such as return on capital employed (ROCE) or return on investment (ROI) are to be calculated (see section 2).

The second one is laid out in the form that most UK companies publish.

The third one is a listing of assets and liabilities (in reverse order to Europe) as typically found in US financial statements.

Balance sheet as at 31 March 2004		Management format	
Fixed assets			
Tangible fixed assets			
Land and property	350		a
Equipment	60		b
		410	c
Intangible fixed assets – goodwill		110	d
Investment fixed assets		20	e
		540	f
Current assets	450		g
Creditors: amounts falling due within one year – (current liabilities)	(389)		h
		61	i
Capital employed			
Total assets less current liabilities		**601**	
Creditors: amounts falling due after more than one year (long term liabilities)		330	j
Shareholders' equity			
Share capital		50	k
Revaluation reserve		114	l
Profit and loss account		107	m
Capital invested		**601**	

Balance sheet as at 31 March 2004   **UK published accounts format**

Fixed assets
Tangible fixed assets

Land and property	350		a
Equipment	60		b
		410	c
Intangible fixed assets – goodwill		110	d
Investment fixed assets		20	e
		540	f
Current assets	450		g
Creditors: amounts falling due in less than one year within one year – (current liabilities)	(389)		h
		61	i

Total assets less current liabilities
capital employed   601   j

Creditors: amounts falling due in less than one
year (long term liabilities)   (330)   j

                                                                    271

Shareholders' equity

Share capital	50	k
Revaluation reserve	114	l
Profit and loss account	107	m
	271	

Balance sheet as at 31 March 2004		US format	
Current assets		450	g
Property, plant and equipment, net		410	c
Other assets	investments,	20	e
	goodwill, net	110	d
Total assets		990	
Current liabilities		389	h
Non current liabilities		330	j
Stockholders' equity			
Common stock	50		k
Revaluation reserve	114		i
Retained earnings	107		m
Total stockholders' equity		271	
Total liabilities and stockholders' equity		990	

Accounting framework

Book keeping with its rigorous arithmetic of pluses and minuses has and does serve well in providing an accounting framework. Business transactions are classified as assets or expenses (debtors/debits) and liabilities to owners or outsiders and income (creditors/credits). The majority of business transactions can be classified correctly.

However, there will be instances where differing views can be taken, e.g. is the purchase of a £2,000 personal computer an immediate expense of the business, to be charged as a debit in the P&L account, or is it and asset of the business to be shown as a fixed asset and capitalized in the balance sheet?

This illustrates the dilemma of whether expenses should be shown as such, or shown as assets. Even with this example most accountants would say there is no big issue. The computers should be capitalized, but then charged as an expense (depreciated) to the P&L account over say, 2 years. There will be valid differences of opinion on the period of charging depreciation (or writing off the asset) but as long as the time period is stated, users of the accounts can understand the figures presented.

Thus, book keeping with sensibly applied guidance on matters as above is a sound framework for producing financial statements. Or is it?

The academic, or rather economist leaning view, is that book keeping is far too simplistic. Assets and liabilities have to be defined in a more robust way.

Assets: *Probable future economic benefits obtained or controlled by a particular entity as a result of past transactions or events.*

Liabilities: *Probable future sacrifices of economic benefits arising from present obligations of a particular entity to transfer assets or provide services to other entities in the future, as a result of past transactions or events.*

Income *is increases in economic benefits during the accounting period in the form of inflows or enhancements of assets or decrease of liabilities that result in increases in equity, other than those relating to contributions from equity participants.*

Expenses *are decreases in economic benefits during an accounting period in the form of outflows or depletions of assets or incurrences of liabilities that result in decreases in equity, other than those relating to distributions to equity participants.*

The IFRS's are all based on a framework which uses such definitions. In aiming to clarify exactly what the nature of an asset or liability is we have definitions that are at times unclear. One laudable aim of defining assets as they are defined is to make the balance sheet more of a 'valuation statement'. However, even here the Standard setters have had to back away or have been caught by their too clever definitions.

Fundamental accounting concepts

Traditionally there were four equally important fundamental concepts:

1 Going concern

2 Accruals or matching

3 Consistency

4 Prudence

On reflection the Standard setters now consider only the first two to be fundamental, consistency and prudence, being relegated to being 'desirable qualities'. This is interesting as one of; if not the prime aim of Accounting Standards is to bring consistency to reporting! That said, it is true that consistency is desirable but not fundamental – it may be appropriate to be inconsistent.

Being 'prudent' is a fundamental concept for those who intend to develop lasting businesses and thus makes sense when accounting for and reporting business transactions. However, the concept can be and has been abused. In good (or even bad!) times one might be too prudent, thus understating profits (or overstating losses!) to allow for 'smoothing' of future results.

The first two 'bedrock' concepts may be defined as follows:

GOING CONCERN

The preparer (and auditor) of the accounts should consider and check whether or not the enterprise is likely to continue in operational existence for the foreseeable future. This means in particular that there is no intention or necessity to liquidate or curtail significantly the scale of operations, and thus the P&L account and balance sheet will not be materially affected.

The 'going concern' concept also requires the preparer (and auditor) to consider and check that the business is likely to have cash/bank resources sufficient to remain in business for the foreseeable future – 'foreseeable future' is considered by UK auditing Standards to be a period of at least twelve months beyond the date of signing the latest year end accounts.

ACCRUALS OR MATCHING CONCEPT

Revenue and costs should be accrued (that is, recognized as they are earned or incurred, not as money is received or paid), matched with one another so far as their relationship can be established or justifiably assumed, and dealt with in the P&L account of the period to which they relate.

The other two concepts may be defined as follows:

CONSISTENCY

There should be consistency of accounting treatment of like items within each accounting period and from one period to the next.

PRUDENCE

Prudence means being cautious. Prudence is the inclusion of a degree of caution in the exercise of judgments needed in making the estimates required under conditions of uncertainty, such that assets or expenses are not overstated and liabilities or expenses are not understated. However, the exercise of prudence does not allow the creation of hidden reserves.

Qualitative characteristics of financial statements

There are many more words used by Standard setters in an attempt to make accounting fit into a clearly defined 'framework'. The following is a list of the terminology/definitions contained in the IASB Framework. At least one of the words is not recognized by spellcheckers! Maybe the Standard setters should acknowledge that accounting is an art and will never be a science!

Most of the words are used as they would be in normal everyday English. Comment is made on the terms that have special significance to accounts preparation.

- Understandability
- Relevance
- Materiality

The concept of materiality is well understood by accountants and auditors but may seem odd to those that believe accounting to be an exact science. What is material? It would be good to, and no doubt most accountants set out with the aim of producing 100% accurate accounts. However, take the example of the year end stock figure. It is carefully counted, damaged goods being identified and eliminated from the count. The stock-take figure totals 89,000, the stock records (adjusted for the damaged stock) show 92,000. What figures should be used? Is the 3,000 difference material? The answer – use the actual lower stock-take figure (this is prudent) and the difference is really not material. IF the difference was say 13,000, then both the stock-take process and the stock records would have to be reviewed.

- **Reliability**
- **Faithful representation**
- **Substance over form**

This is most important, and if followed rigorously Enron may not have happened! It means that it is the underlying business position that matters, not the legal form. For example, equipment may be leased over 5 years – 60 monthly instalments being paid; ownership of the equipment legally remains with the bank financing the equipment; BUT the substance of the transaction is that the equipment is 'owned', that is the economic benefits of ownership flow to the lessee. Equally the bank does not really consider it owns equipment – it has lent money to be repaid in 60 instalments.

- Neutrality
- Completeness
- Comparability

Constraints are acknowledged:
- timeliness;
- balance between benefit and cost;
- balance between qualitative characteristics; and
- true and fair view/fair presentation.

If there are profits there must be cash, uses of cash

If a business consistently generates profits from trading then there must be cash flowing into the business. However, this does not mean that the business will necessarily end up with a cash mountain – it depends on how cash generated is consumed or spent.

Cash could be spent on stocks or to fund debtors – cash could be tied up in working capital. Cash could be invested in tangible fixed assets or investments. Cash could be distributed to the owners as dividends.

It is seldom the case that the profit for a year equals the cash balance available at the end of the year. For businesses both large and small, it is generally considered wrong to have cash mountains, either the cash should be invested in fixed assets and working capital to make the business grow, or returned to the owners for them to invest elsewhere.

Conversely, if a business makes a loss it does not necessarily follow that in the short-term there will be no cash. However, if a business continues to make losses over a number of years then unless there are injections of new funds into the business there will be an increasing cash deficit and ultimately the company will become insolvent.

Cash flow statements

For a proper understanding of a business it is vital to understand where cash came from and where it is being consumed. A reconciliation between opening and closing cash, bank and borrowing balances is needed. A cash flow statement aims to reveal such information.

CASH FLOW STATEMENTS – A VERY SIMPLE ILLUSTRATION

The profit and loss account for a business for the year ended 31 March 2004 shows that the business has made a profit of 3,000. It might be expected that as this is a very simple and straightforward business there will be a cash or bank balance of 3,000.

Profit and loss account for the period ended 31 March 2004	
Sales	30,000
Expenses	(25,000)
Depreciation	(2,000)
Profit	**3,000**

However, not all business transactions are *for cash* that is paid or received as cash immediately. In this illustration 6,000 of sales have been made to a customer *on credit*, Similarly 1,500 of expenses do not have to be paid for until the next accounting year. The 2,000 charge for depreciation is a cost of consuming or using a van, but there is no cash payment in respect of this cost. The cash flows in respect of a van occur when it is purchased or finally disposed of.

Maybe more significantly, not all the cash transactions which a business undertakes relate to purchasing or selling goods or services, or paying for expenses – not all cash movements are related to P&L movements. Many cash transactions will be in respect of purchasing or selling assets, or incurring or settling liabilities – they will be related to movements or changes in balance sheet items.

In this simple illustration the business has also taken out a 9,000 loan during the year and spent 8,000 on the purchase of a van.

Cash flow statement for the year ended 31 March 2004

Inflows		
	loan	9,000
	from sales	24,000
Outflows	expenses paid	(23,500)
	purchase of van	(8,000)
	net cash inflow	**1,500**

The net effect of the differences between occurrence of P&L transactions and the receipt or payment of cash, plus the other balance sheet movements in cash, is that in this simple illustration the business has a closing cash balance of 1,500 rather than 3,000 which is the profit figure. The principal reason is of course the 6,000 outstanding from customers.

Cash flow statements do not require additional record keeping, they may be produced by identifying the movements between the beginning and ending balance sheets, (adjusting for non-cash movements) – the indirect method and the one most commonly used in practice. They can also be prepared by appropriately summarizing and classifying cash book entries – the direct method.

An illustration in the preparation of a cash flow statement is set out overleaf.

Balance sheet as at 31 December 2003

		2003		2002
Tangible fixed assets note 1		74,800		53,400
Current assets				
Stock	22,500		14,600	
Debtors	31,600		15,400	
Cash	2,200		1,300	
	56,300		31,300	
Current liabilities				
Overdraft	(13,900)		(1,900)	
Trade Creditors	(23,600)		(19,800)	
Taxation	(8,700)		(1,700)	
	(46,200)		(23,400)	
Net current assets		10,100		7,900
Total assets less current liabilities		84,900		61,300
Creditors: amounts falling due after more than one year				
Bank loan		(15,000)		(10,000)
		69,900		51,300
Called up share capital		20,000		20,000
Profit and loss account		49,900		31,300
		69,900		51,300

Note 1

	Land & buildings	Fixtures & fittings	Motor vehicles	Totals
Cost				
at 1.1.03	51,100	5,500	0	56,600
Additions	0	16,000	9,200	25,200
at 31.12.03	51,100	21,500	9,200	81,800
Accumulated depreciation				
at 1.1.03	0	3,200	0	3,200
Charge for year	0	1,500	2,300	3,800
at 31.12.03	0	4,700	2,300	7,000
Net book amount				
at 1.1.03	51,100	2,300	0	53,400
at 31.12.03	51,000	16,800	6,900	74,800

Note 2

For simplicity, the only profit is the operating profit for the year, being the movement on the profit and loss account.

Profit and loss account for the year ended

		2003		2002
Sales		210,000		198,000
Cost of sales		(105,100)		(102,400)
Gross profit		95,900		95,600
admin costs	(62,600)		(58,700)	
depreciation	(3,800)		(1,600)	
		(66,400)		(60,300)
Operating profit		29,500		35,300
Interest charge		(1,400)		(1,150)
Profit before tax		28,100		34,150
Taxation		(7,500)		(9,200)
Profit available for shareholders		20,600		24,950
Dividend paid		(2,000)		(18,000)
Profit retained		18,600		6,950
Profit brought forward		31,300		24,350
Profit carried forward		**49,900**		**31,300**

Inflows and outflows of funds

	Inflows	Outflows
Profit	29,500	
Depreciation	3,800	not a cash flow
Loans	5,000	
Stocks		7,900
Debtors		16,200
Creditors	3,800	
Taxation (paid)		500
Purchase of fixed assets		25,200
Interest paid		1,400
Dividend paid		2,000
	42,100	53,200
Net outflow	**-11,100**	

Change in cash and bank

Decrease in cash	900
Increase in overdraft	-12,000
	-11,100

Cash flow statement for the year ended 31 December 2003

Cash flows from operating activities

Cash generated from operations	**13,000**	note 3
Interest paid	(1,400)	
Tax paid	(500)	

Net cash from operating activities		**11,100**

Cash flows from/(to) investing activities

Purchase of fixed assets		(25,200)

Cash flows from financing activities

Increase in long term loan	5,000	
Dividends paid	(2,000)	
these could be shown under operating activities		

		3,000
Net (decrease)/increase in cash equivalents		**(11,100)**

Net (decrease)/increase in cash equivalents

Opening cash	1,300	
Opening cash	2,200	
		900
Opening overdraft	1,900	
Closing overdraft	13,900	
		(12,000)
		(11,100)

Note 3: Cash generated by operating activities

Profit per accounts	29,500
Add back depreciation	3,800
Changes in working capital	
stock	(7,900)
debtors	(16,200)
creditors	3,800
Cash flow from operating activities	13,000

Accounting ratios

This section reviews principal accounting ratios and comments, where appropriate, how poor accounting may distort the ratios and where the Standards may affect the ratios.

Balance sheet ratios

GEARING RATIOS

There are two commonly used ratios that tell us how much borrowing a company has, how highly 'Geared' it is.

THE GEARING RATIO

The gearing ratio = $\dfrac{\text{Long-term loans (or borrowings of whatever kind)}}{\text{Shareholders' funds + long-term loans}}$

$$= \text{(capital employed or invested)}$$

This is the more common definition of gearing for a company and levels might be considered as follows:

0%-20% – Low gearing: It would be expected that most companies will have some borrowings and levels up to 20% are modest.

20%-35% – Medium gearing: A normal level for many companies. Loans will be regularly taken out and repaid as the company invests in new assets or new business ventures. A company should be very clear as to why it has borrowings of, say, 31% – this level of gearing should not just happen!

35%-50% – High gearing: This level of borrowing may be more applicable to some businesses than others, e.g. an investment property company would normally be highly geared due to the very significant investment in tangible fixed assets and more important still, the ability to repay loans from inflows from rental income. Gearing of this level requires careful management. When a company is 50%+ geared, the shareholders should ask, 'Whose company is it?'. The company is certainly answerable (if not owned by) the banks.

Gearing may also be expressed by:

Debt to equity ratio = $\dfrac{\text{Long-term loans}}{\text{Shareholders' funds}}$

This is often the way banks express gearing. The numbers will be of a different order.

e.g. 50% gearing = 1 to 1 debt/equity ratio. The message conveyed by the ratio will be as for the gearing ratio.

HOW CAN GEARING BE MISREPRESENTED?

Method	Standard that aims to prevent this
Miss-classifying loans and equity	IAS 32 and IAS 39 on financial instruments. IAS 30 on disclosure for banks
Off balance sheet finance	IAS 17 leases
Not consolidating subsidiaries	Reliance on the concept of substance over form in the IAS framework.

Working capital and gearing ratios

A business has to meet its obligations as they fall due, or it may go bust! The business must have sufficient working capital. Working capital or liquidity ratios attempt to measure a company's ability to meet its short-term obligations as they fall due.

Current ratio = $\dfrac{\text{Current Assets}}{\text{Current Liabilities}}$

The current ratio is calculated by dividing current assets by current liabilities. Current assets are cash and assets expected to be converted into cash within one year (e.g. WIP, stock and debtors); current liabilities are those that must be paid within one year (e.g. overdrafts, creditors and taxation). A business ought to be able to meet its current obligations if current assets exceed current liabilities. Textbooks traditionally quote this ratio as having to be 2:1 or better if a company was to be sound and able to pay its way. This might be true for a 'typical' business but many company's have ratios of less than 2:1 and are still able to meet their debts when they fall due. Much depends on the industry sector and size of business, e.g. a large supermarket chain might have only 12 days stock – this will be recorded at cost, but not pay its suppliers (of the stock) for 60 days, a super market could have negative working capital and a current ratio of less than 1:1.

Liquidity ratio/quick ratio/acid test ratio =

$$\frac{\text{Current assets} - \text{stock or WIP}}{\text{Current liabilities}}$$

Current assets include stock/WIP which is often not readily converted into cash. The liquidity ratio has stock/WIP taken out of the numerator. This provides a more rigorous test of the company's ability to settle its obligations as they fall due. Textbooks traditionally quote this ratio as having to be 1:1 or better, if a company is to survive! That is, its cash like assets (Debtors and Cash) must equal its current (immediately due) liabilities. There is a logic to this, but the ratio appropriate to a business will again very much depend on the type of business.

Method	Standard that aims to prevent this
Over or under stating components of working capital: stock, debtors, cash or creditors	Individual Standards that deal with items e.g. IAS 2 Inventories
By 'window dressing', that is netting off items or miss classifying them	IAS framework

Performance measures

RATIO ANALYSIS

How do you measure the performance of a business?

The first measure that normally comes to mind is profitability – the business must make a profit.

Another measure – does the business generate positive cash flows, or at least sufficient cash to survive? This is important for all companies, but particularly listed companies as there is a need to pay regular cash dividends. Many analysts get too focused on one type of measure. For example, in the last few years there has been focus on ebitda (earnings before interest, tax, depreciation and amortization). It is a measure of cash generation BUT there is still the underlying need to make profit – revenues must exceed expenses over the long-term!

Another measure of performance may be seen as efficient use of assets – how well does the business use its assets – do the managers 'make the assets sweat'.

There are also many non-financial measures of performance which may well have an effect on the level of financial performance. For example, staff turnover or the frequency of environmental law infringements.

The need to make an adequate return

The prime measure of a businesses success, or not, is the level of return on the capital employed (ROCE) or return on investment (ROI). It is a ratio of the profit the business makes, divided by the capital employed needed to deliver the profit.

An example: 100,000 is invested in plant and machinery, stock, etc., and this can be used to manufacture and sell items, the profit at the end of a period, divided by the 100,000 will be the return on the capital invested or employed. This is similar to having 100,000 invested in a bank deposit account earning interest – say 9,800 over a period of a year, the return on capital invested or employed is:

$$\frac{9,800}{100,000} \quad = \quad 9.8\%$$

Return on Capital Employed = $\dfrac{\textbf{Net Operating Profit}}{\textbf{Capital Employed}}$

Net operating profit is normally taken as net operating profit of the ordinary on-going business before interest and taxation.

Capital employed is taken as the year end or average capital employed, in generating the profit.

It is obvious that return on capital employed could be calculated either before or after tax and interest. The figure which is used for calculation will depend very much on the reasons for looking at returns. For example, a shareholder interested in the return their company is giving may well only be concerned with profit after tax and interest. If it is performance measure that one is looking for, the profit before tax and interest is a clear indication of profit derived from using assets. Interest and taxation are related to other issues, the interest paid will depend on the financial structure of the company and the taxation dependent on the tax regime ruling at the time, or in the country concerned.

As most managers will be concerned with comparing their operating performance year by year they will not want this clouded by issues such as interest or tax payments.

In the following examples return on capital employed is considered to be:

$$\frac{\text{net operating profit (before interest and tax)}}{\text{capital employed}}$$

This gives a clearer and more consistent method of comparing companies – bench-marking.

As an illustration, we will take a company which has a return on capital employed of 20%. This is the prime ratio and this, the ratio analysis, splits up into two clear sub ratios and thus types of analysis.

$$\textbf{ROCE} = \frac{\textbf{net operating profit}\ \text{(before interest and tax)}}{\text{capital employed}}$$

net profit % =

$\dfrac{\textbf{net operating profit}}{\textbf{sales or turnover}}$	$\dfrac{\textbf{sales or turnover}}{\textbf{capital employed}}$	= asset turnover

The left hand ratio is called the **net profit percent**. The definition of net operating profit should be the same as that used for the calculation of return on capital employed and sales is the figure of net sales or turnover received in a year. The net profit % is the total sales less all labor, material, overhead costs. A net profit of 10% will be used as an example, although the rate of net profit will very much depend on the type of industry concerned.

The right hand ratio is called the **asset turnover ratio** or asset utilization ratio (AUR). This is a ratio of:

$$\frac{\text{sales or turnover (as defined in net profit\%)}}{\text{capital employed (as defined in return on capital employed)}}$$

This ratio is expressed as a multiple, 3:1, 5:1, 10:1, rather than 300%, 500% or 1,000%. It is a measure of what sales activity (what movement of goods or services) one gets from the capital employed. Obviously, a higher multiple is seen as being more efficient but the multiple will very much depend on the type of industry being analyzed. For instance, an engineering company, with high amounts of capital employed invested in plant and machinery would typically have a low multiple, 2:1 being quite common, whereas a service company, often with very little capital employed would have a high multiple, say, 4:1. Whatever the type of business, the drive will always be to produce a higher multiple as this affects the return on capital employed – the primary ratio.

Once these two subsidiary ratios have been calculated, it can be seen that the:

Net Profit % x Asset Turnover = Return on Capital Employed.

It is important to be aware of this arithmetical link. For example, if net profit % falls due to the market place competition, one way of maintaining returns would be to become more efficient, that is, to increase sales from the capital employed used ('make the assets sweat') or reduce the capital employed. This is not surprising and it is manifested in the common practice of out-sourcing or sub-contracting. The aim is to reduce capital employed at every turn – reduce tangible fixed assets – buildings, shops, equipment employed – and keep levels of stocks and debtors well under control.

OVERHEAD OR EXPENSE ANALYSIS

Further ratios under net profit % are obtained from an analysis of the overhead or expense headings, for example, wages to sales; motor costs to sales; heat and light or occupancy costs to sales; telephone/fax costs to sales, etc. These ratios are used throughout industries for control purposes.

ASSET TURNOVER

A further analysis of asset turnover is given by looking at turnover or sales to fixed assets; turnover or sales to stock; turnover or sales to debtor; turnover or sales or, more correctly, cost of sales to creditors.

Method	Standard that aims to prevent this
Understating capital employed	IAS 17 leases, IAS's 22 and 27 consolidated accounts. Many Standards require assets to be shown at fair value
	BUT Goodwill cannot be revalued also revaluation of tangible fixed assets is not compulsory so capital employed may well be understated
Overstating profit	IAS 18 Revenue should be earned thus profits should be real

Stock market measures

Another area of performance measurement is that of measuring the perform-ance of a company by its performance in relation to other listed or quoted companies – how does it perform in relation to the market?

The following terms and ratios are the principal ones used when considering stock market performance.

Share values

There are three share values commonly quoted and they are as follows:

1   Nominal (par) value

2   Book (asset) value

3   Market value

NOMINAL (PAR) VALUE

The nominal value is largely a notional low figure arbitrarily placed on a company's stock. It serves to determine the value of 'issued common stock'.

BOOK VALUE

This value is arrived at by dividing the number of issued shares into the owners' funds.

MARKET VALUE (MARKET CAPITALIZATION IS THE MARKET VALUE TIMES THE NUMBER OF SHARES IN ISSUE)

This is the price quoted in the Stock Exchange for a public company or an estimated price for a non-quoted company. On the Stock Exchange the figure changes daily in response to actual or anticipated results and overall sentiment of the market.

Earnings per share (EPS)

Earnings per share is one of the most widely quoted performance measures when there is a discussion of a company's performance or share value. The profit used in the calculation is the profit available to shareholders after all other claimants have been satisfied. The most common prior charges in the profit and loss account are interest and tax. The profit is divided by the number of issued shares to calculate the value of earnings per share. This figure tells us what profit has been earned by the shareholder for every share held. There is an Accounting Standard which further defines profit and number of shares as it may be possible to manipulate these figures.

One important piece of additional information is that the 'fully diluted' EPS should be shown. Fully diluted means that if all options on shares, to directors, employees or to those holders of loans which can be converted into ordinary shares were taken up then obviously the number of shares in existence would increase and the EPS figure would fall. A much lower fully diluted EPS figure indicates many options in existence or a high level of convertible loans.

Note: IAS 33 Earnings per share aims to prevent manipulation of this important ratio.

DIVIDEND COVER

This is a ratio of profits available for ordinary shareholders expressed as a multiple of the total dividends paid and payable.

EARNINGS YIELD AND DIVIDEND YIELD

The yield on a share can be expressed as the return it provides in terms of earnings or dividends as a percentage of the current share price.

PRICE TO EARNINGS RATIO (PE RATIO)

The price to earnings ratio is a widely quoted measure of share value. The share price is divided by the EPS figure.

MARKET TO BOOK RATIO

The ratio relates the total market capitalization of the company to the shareholders' funds.

9.3

Creative accounting

One of the prime aims of the Standards is to prevent creative accounting. Thus, what is shown here should not occur in practice. The purpose of this chapter is to help readers understand some of the methods that have been (or might still be) used to manipulate or miss-represent financial statements and the figures therein.

How can financial statements be distorted?

Quite easily:

- Over-stated good news   under-stated bad news
- Over-stated asset and   under-stated liabilities and
  income amounts   expenses

Some examples:

Motives/drivers	Affect what?	How?
Higher profits/pay higher dividends	Profits	Increase sales Decrease costs Classify unrealized profits as realized
Increase company value	Balance sheet net worth	Increase asset values Decrease/hide liabilities
Deliver better returns	Balance sheet capital employed. Profit	Take assets and the contra liabilities off balance sheet. Increase profits
Improve cash flows	Cash and bank balances, debtors and creditors	Withhold payments

Probably the most common abuses are to ignore the matching concept – bring income in early or leave costs un-accrued, treat expenses as assets – capitalize costs as tangible fixed assets.

Another means of being creative with figures is to omit figures altogether – especially to take assets, and thus the contra liabilities, off the balance sheet. Two common methods are outlined below. Omitting leased assets and the associated liabilities and not consolidating subsidiaries. Again, it must be stated that the Standards, properly applied should prevent such practices.

9.4
Off balance sheet items – the issues

There are two main issues in practice. Understatement of the capital employed and understatement of the liabilities of a business. The former is important as assets effectively owned and certainly managed by the business are omitted, the latter as real liabilities of the business are omitted – they are off the balance sheet that is hidden.

Omitting off balance sheet assets and liabilities results in distortion of important performance measures such as return on investment (ROI) and gearing.

Leased assets – an example

A   The apparent position ignoring the leased assets and the liability to the leasing company

The contention is that the lease charges are simply expenses to be paid as incurred. The example shows lease charges of 125 per year and minimal depreciation related to the 8 of equipment shown. The apparent return is 24% and gearing is 25%.

Balance sheet as at 21 March 2004   **A**

Tangible fixed assets

	Land and property		200
	Equipment	a	8
			208

Net current assets – working capital | | | 70 |

Total assets less current liabilities

Capital employed | | b | **278** |

Financed by:
Creditors: amounts falling due after more
than one year (long term liabilities) | | c | 70 |

Shareholders equity

Share capital	50		
Profit and loss account	158	d	
			208
		e	**278**

Profit and loss account for the year ended 31 March 2004 – extract

Operating profit for year before depreciation	f	200
Leasing charges	g	(125)
Depreciation/amortisation charge	h	(2)
Interest/finance charge	i	(5)
Net operating profit before taxation	j	68

Return on capital employed (ROCE) =

$$\frac{\text{operating profit for year}}{\text{capital employed}} \quad \frac{i}{\text{bore}} \quad \frac{68}{278} \ = \ 24\%$$

Gearing =

$$\frac{\text{long term abilities}}{\text{+ Long term liabilities}} \quad \frac{c}{e} \quad \frac{70}{278} \ = \ 25\%$$

B   However, what should the accounts really show?

The equipment is leased for a period of 3 years minimum (the company is committed to rent the equipment and make the 36 monthly payments). The arms length cost of the equipment was 300,000 when purchased at the beginning of the year.

In substance the company is purchasing the equipment over 3 years. At the end of the first year the equipment would be written down to 200,000 (100,000 depreciation charge). A portion of the 'loan' of 300,000 at the start of the year would be repaid and there would be an interest charge on the loan. If the real substance of the transactions is recorded then the return on capital actually employed falls to 13% and the gearing when the loan liabilities are included is 58%

Note: The figures are approximations of what would really pertain; it is the effect of off balance sheet leasing that is important.

Balance sheet as at 21 March 2004

Tangible fixed assets		
Land and property		200
Equipment	a	<u>208</u>
		408
Net current assets – working capital		70
Total assets less current liabilities		
Capital employed	b	**478**

Financed by:
Creditors: amounts falling due after more
than one year (long term liabilities)   c   277

Shareholders equity			
Share capital	50		
Profit and loss account	<u>158</u>	d	
			<u>201</u>
		e	**478**

Profit and loss account for the year ended 31 March 2004 – extract

Operating profit for year before depreciation	f	200
Leasing charges	g	0
Depreciation/amortisation charge	h	(102)
Interest/finance charge	i	(37)
Net operating profit before taxation	j	61

Return on capital employed (ROCE) =

operating profit for year	i	<u>61</u>	=	**13%**
capital employed	bore	478		

Gearing =

long term abilities	c	<u>277</u>	=	**58%**
Shareholders' equity	e	478		
+ Long term liabilities				

In summary

The reasons for removing assets from the balance sheet are two fold.

The first is to reduce borrowing and thus apparent levels of gearing.

The second is to reduce apparent capital employed and thus increase the return on capital employed ratio. This gives the impression that the business is performing better than it really is.

Reducing apparent levels of borrowing is one of the principal reasons for PFI (Private Financial Initiatives) PPP (Public Private partnerships). This approach to funding public assets is popular with governments of whatever persuasion – they borrow less. The principal benefit of PFI or PPP is held to be that the private sector will be more efficient at building and operating assets than government bureaucracies. This may well be true but it does not alter the fact that governments are committing citizens to the liability of having to spend cash over a number of years. The governments are indirectly borrowing money, at possibly higher rates than those at which sound governments could borrow. Just like their private sector counterparts governments want to impress with the illusion of low borrowing.

Consolidating subsidiaries – an example

A group of companies has a parent or holding company that owns investments in one or more subsidiary companies. The parent company may trade
in its own name, but frequently the parent is primarily an investment company.
A balance sheet for such a parent company (A) is shown below:

PARENT

Balance sheet as at 31 March 2004			**A**
Fixed assets			
Investment fixed assets		20	e
Current assets	45		g
Creditors: amounts falling due, within one year (current liabilities)	(39)		h
		6	i
Capital employed Total assets less current liabilities		26	j
Creditors: amounts falling due after more than one year (long term liabilities)		2	k
Stockholders' equity			
Share capital		10	m
Profit and loss account		14	o
		26	p

If there was no requirement to consolidate and produce group or consolidated accounts then shareholders and other interested parties would have
to gather together the accounts for the parent and subsidiaries, and combine
them to get an overall view. In this example, the parent A has one subsidiary
B shown below. Note: B has a significantly higher amount of assets and liabilities than the parent A.

Balance sheet as at 31 March 2004			**B**
Fixed assets			
Tangible fixed assets			
Land and property	150		a
Equipment – **leased**	<u>260</u>		b
		410	c
Current assets	341		g
Creditors: amounts falling due, within one year (current liabilities)	<u>(290)</u>		h
		<u>51</u>	i
Capital employed Total assets less current liabilities		<u>**461**</u>	j
Creditors: amounts falling due after more than one year (long term liabilities)		440	k
Stockholders' equity			
Share capital		20	m
Profit and loss account		<u>1</u>	o
		<u>**461**</u>	p

Company law in the UK and most countries (supported by Standards IAS 22 and IAS 27) requires that a set of group or consolidated accounts are produced at each year end. Note: the accounting records for the business transactions are held in the parent and subsidiaries accounts. Accounts have to be produced for these entities. The group accounts are a year end creation. In simple terms the figures are added together, but with the elimination of the investment of the parent against the equity of the subsidiary – otherwise there would be double-counting!

The process for this simple example is shown below and the group balance sheet (C) is produced.

Balance sheet as at 31 March 2004

	Parent		Subsidiary		
Fixed assets					
Tangible fixed assets					
Land and property	0	a	150		
Equipment	0	b	260		
Tangible fixed assets		0	c	410	410
Current assets	45	g	341		
Creditors: amounts falling due, within one year (current liabilities)	(39)	h	(290)		
		6	i	51	57
Capital employed Total assets less current liabilities		26	j	461	467
Creditors: amounts falling due after more than one year (long term liabilities)		2	k	440	442
Stockholders' equity					
Share capital		10	m		10
Profit and loss account		14	o	1	15
		26	p	461	467

One way of hiding assets and maybe more significantly the contra liabilities is NOT to consolidate subsidiaries. This was part of the Enron scam. Entities that were controlled by the parent Enron were owned in a devious fashion in special purpose vehicles that meant they did not appear to be wholly owned subsidiaries and thus assets and huge amounts of liabilities – debt were left off Enron's balance sheet.

Other titles from Thorogood

THE FINANCE AND ACCOUNTING DESKTOP GUIDE

Ralph Tiffin

£16.99 paperback, ISBN 1 85418 121 1

Published October 1998

Understanding finance and applying techniques for financial control are essential for successful management, yet in many cases key financial and accounting tools are either unknown or unsuccessfully applied. This Desktop Guide provides a clear, practical guide to all aspects of accountancy, financial and business literacy.

COMPANY DIRECTOR'S DESKTOP GUIDE

David Martin

£16.99 paperback, ISBN 1 85418 294 3

Published June 2004

The role of the company director is fundamental to the success of any business, yet the tasks, responsibilities and liabilities that directors' face become more demanding with every change to the law.

Written in a clear, jargon-free style, this is a comprehensive guide to the complex legislation and procedures governing all aspects of the company director's role. The author's wide experience as a Director and Secretary of a plc and consultant and author provides a manual that is expert, practical and easy to access.

THE COMPANY SECRETARY'S DESKTOP GUIDE

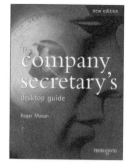

Roger Mason
£16.99 paperback, ISBN 1 85418 284 6
Published April 2004

Written in a clear, jargon-free style, this is a comprehensive guide to the complex legislation and procedures
governing all aspects of the company secretary's work.
The Company Secretary's role becomes more demanding
with every change to the law and practice. The author's
considerable experience as both Company Secretary and lecturer and author
has ensured a manual that is expert, practical and easy to access.

THE CREDIT CONTROLLER'S DESKTOP GUIDE

Proven procedures and techniques for getting paid on
time and preserving cash

Roger Mason
£16.99 paperback, ISBN 1 85418 299 4
Published September 2004

Clear and jargon-free, this is an expert and practical
guide to the techniques of effective credit control. This
book takes account of all the recent changes to the law and practice, including:
winding up, bankruptcy, receivership and administration, following imple-
mentation of The Enterprise Act 2002; statutory interest; obtaining judgment
for unpaid debts; the abolition of Crown Preference and the effect on ordinary
creditors; new rules concerning the recovery of VAT when there is a bad debt;
what is available from Companies House; the latest thinking on retention of
title clauses in conditions of sale.

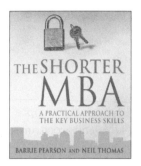

THE SHORTER MBA

A practical approach to the key business skills

Barrie Pearson and Neil Thomas
£35.00 Hardback, ISBN 1 85418 305 2
Published July 2004

A succinct distillation of the skills that you need to be successful in business. Most people can't afford to give up two years to study for an MBA. This pithy, practical book presents all the essential theory, practiced and techniques taught to MBA students – ideal for the busy practising executive. It is divided into three parts:

* Personal development

* Management skills

* Business development

SUCCESSFUL BUSINESS PLANNING

Norton Paley
£14.99 paperback, £29.99 hardback
Published June 2004

"Growth firms with a written business plan have increased their revenues 69 per cent faster over the past five years than those without a written plan."

FROM A SURVEY BY PRICEWATERHOUSECOOPERS

We know the value of planning – in theory. But either we fail to spend the time required to go through the thinking process properly, or we fail to use the plan effectively. Paley uses examples from real companies to turn theory into practice.

BUSINESS SEMINARS

Focused on developing your potential

Falconbury, the sister company to Thorogood publishing, brings together the leading experts from all areas of management and strategic development to provide you with a comprehensive portfolio of action-centred training and learning.

We understand everything managers and leaders need to be, know and do to succeed in today's commercial environment. Each product addresses a different technical or personal development need that will encourage growth and increase your potential for success.

- Practical public training programmes
- Tailored in-company training
- Coaching
- Mentoring
- Topical business seminars
- Trainer bureau/bank
- Adair Leadership Foundation

The most valuable resource in any organization is its people; it is essential that you invest in the development of your management and leadership skills to ensure your team fulfil their potential. Investment into both personal and professional development has been proven to provide an outstanding ROI through increased productivity in both you and your team. Ultimately leading to a dramatic impact on the bottom line.

With this in mind Falconbury have developed a comprehensive portfolio of training programmes to enable managers of all levels to develop their skills in leadership, communications, finance, people management, change management and all areas vital to achieving success in today's commercial environment.

What Falconbury can offer you?

- Practical applied methodology with a proven results
- Extensive bank of experienced trainers
- Limited attendees to ensure one-to-one guidance
- Up to the minute thinking on management and leadership techniques
- Interactive training
- Balanced mix of theoretical and practical learning
- Learner-centred training
- Excellent cost/quality ratio

Falconbury In-Company Training

Falconbury are aware that a public programme may not be the solution to leadership and management issues arising in your firm. Involving only attendees from your organization and tailoring the programme to focus on the current challenges you face individually and as a business may be more appropriate. With this in mind we have brought together our most motivated and forward thinking trainers to deliver tailored in-company programmes developed specifically around the needs within your organization.

All our trainers have a practical commercial background and highly refined people skills. During the course of the programme they act as facilitator, trainer and mentor, adapting their style to ensure that each individual benefits equally from their knowledge to develop new skills.

Falconbury works with each organization to develop a programme of training that fits your needs.

Mentoring and coaching

Developing and achieving your personal objectives in the workplace is becoming increasingly difficult in today's constantly changing environment. Additionally, as a manager or leader, you are responsible for guiding colleagues towards the realization of their goals. Sometimes it is easy to lose focus on your short and long-term aims.

Falconbury's one-to-one coaching draws out individual potential by raising self-awareness and understanding, facilitating the learning and performance development that creates excellent managers and leaders. It builds renewed self-confidence and a strong sense of 'can-do' competence, contributing significant benefit to the organization. Enabling you to focus your energy on developing your potential and that of your colleagues.

Mentoring involves formulating winning strategies, setting goals, monitoring achievements and motivating the whole team whilst achieving a much improved work life balance.

Falconbury – Business Legal Seminars

Falconbury Business Legal Seminars specializes in the provision of high quality training for legal professionals from both in-house and private practice internationally.

The focus of these events is to provide comprehensive and practical training on current international legal thinking and practice in a clear and informative format.

Event subjects include, drafting commercial agreements, employment law, competition law, intellectual property, managing an in-house legal department and international acquisitions.

For more information on all our services please contact Falconbury on +44 (0) 20 7729 6677 or visit the website at: www.falconbury.co.uk